DESPERATE DISGUISES

Living in the Shadow of Psychiatric Illness

Jo Clancy, LMSW-ACP, LCDC

PSYCHOSOCIAL PRESS

Madison   Connecticut

Library of Congress Cataloging-in-Publication Data

Clancy, Jo.
    Desperate disguises : living in the shadow of psychiatric illness / Jo Clancy.
      p.   cm.
    ISBN 1-887841-09-1
    1. Mental illness—Popular works.   I. Title.
  RC454.4.C55   1998
  616.89—dc21

                                         97-21397
                                          CIP

Manufactured in the United States of America

DESPERATE DISGUISES

For Linda: my sister and forever friend

CONTENTS

Acknowledgments   xiii

Preface   xv

Part I: Beliefs Create Reality
Chapter 1 Social Attitudes: The Silent Killer   3
    Statement 1: "The Mentally Ill Are Crazy Psycho-
        Killers Who Should Be Locked Away Forever"   7
    Statement 2: "They Are an Embarrassment to Soci-
        ety and Should Be Hidden Away Forever"   9
    Statement 3: "They Isolate Themselves Because
        They Don't Really Want to Be a Part of Society" 10
    Statement 4: "They Aren't Very Smart People"   12
    Statement 5: "People with Mental Illnesses Are Be-
        ing Punished by God"   12
    Statement 6: "People with Mental Illnesses Are Not
        Like the Rest of Us"   13
    Statement 7: "I Don't Think It Really Exists; I
        Think People Just Say They Have Mental Prob-
        lems to Get Out of Working"   15

Chapter 2 Understanding Mental Illness   19
    Assigning a Label   21
    The Issue of Intensity   22
    The Issue of Duration   23
    The Issue of Single or Recurrent Symptoms   24
    Single vs. Dual Diagnosis   25

The Hardware Man   25
The Wrong Chart   27
The Antisocial with a Heart   28
The Compassionate Alcoholic   29
The Upbeat Schizophrenic   30
A Card with Love   31
The Diaper Bag   31
The Wall   32

Part II: The Deadly Masquerade
Chapter 3 The Picture of Health   37
The Bride   41
The Glamour of Hollywood   42
What's Your "Outer Limit"?   44
The Hologram   45
The Broken Thermos   46
The Self-Cleaning Oven   47
The Alien   48

Chapter 4 The Caveman   51
Sleeping Bears   54
Suspended Animation   56
The Mirage   57
The Soundproof Room   58
Buried Alive   59
The Lost Child   60

Chapter 5 Tears of a Clown   63
The Mascot   66
Tickle Torture   67
Sitcom Mania   68
Halloween Goblins   70
The Stand-Up Comic   71

Chapter 6 The Porcupine   75
The Angry Man   76

The Quiet Man   78
The Prickly Pear   79
The Ladder   81
The Bull   83
The Octopus   84
The Desperate Struggle   85
The Steel Trap   86
Those Eyes   87

Chapter 7 The Warrior   89
Pregnant and Dying   93
Mistaken Identity   93
The Family   94
Craps, You Lose   95
Dear Friends   96
The Promise   96

Chapter 8 The Ugly Duckling   99
The Misfit   100
The Warthog   102
Bird Legs   103
Ignorance Can Be Deadly   105
The Mirror   107

Chapter 9 The Price We All Pay   111
My Brother, My Son   115
If I Die Before I Wake   117
I'm So Happy I Could Just Die   119

Chapter 10 Barriers to Change   121
Negative Social Attitudes about Mental Illness   122
The Engineer   123
The Maze Without End   124
Fear of Rejection/Abandonment   125
Learning Boundaries   126
The Absence of Effective Coping Skills   127

Exhaustion   128
    Too Tired to Care   129
Learned Helplessness   130

Part III: On Becoming Real
Chapter 11 Dying to Be Real   135
    The Man Who Could Not Die   136
    Trapped in the Pages   138
    The Walking Wounded   140

Chapter 12 Awareness: The First Step   143
    The Hungry Dog   144
    Risk Factors   147
        Negative Thoughts   147
        Negative Feelings   148
        Tunnel Vision   148
        Negative Self-Esteem   149
        Peer Pressure to Conform   149
        Unrealistic Expectations   150
        Social Isolation   151
        Desire to Test the Limits/Denial   151
        Shame   152
        Self-Pity   153
        Impatience   154
        Self-Medicating   155
        Loss of Daily Structure   156
        Other Focused   157
        Success and Happy Feelings   158
        Holidays, Special Occasions, Anniversary Dates 158
        Relationship Conflicts   159
        Changes in Sleep, Diet, or Exercise Patterns   160
    Not for Patients Only!   161

Chapter 13 Tools for Your Toolbox   163
    Sixteen Tools for Your Toolbox   165
        1. Identifying Personal Risk Factors   165

2. Monitoring for Change   165
3. Allow Others to Provide Objective Feedback   166
4. Develop a Support Network   167
5. When in Doubt, Call in the Experts!   168
6. Avoid Illicit Drugs, Alcohol, and Prescription Drug Abuse   168
7. Add Structure to Your Life   169
8. Devise a Self-Care Plan   170
9. Acquire a Wide Range of Coping Skills   173
10. Reevaluate Skills on a Regular Basis   174
11. Get Help to Manage Family Conflicts   174
12. Realize You Are Grieving a Loss   175
13. Be Prepared for Things to Get Worse Before
    They Get Better   175
14. Patience is a Virtue   176
15. Keep on Talking   177
16. Celebrate Successes Along the Way   177

Chapter 14 A Work in Progress   181

Epilogue   187

Suggested Reading List   189
    Anxiety and Panic Disorders   189
    Child and Adolescent Disorders   190
    Dual Diagnosis   191
    Major Depression/Manic Depression (Bipolar
        Disorder)   191
    Miscellaneous Topics   192
    Obsessive-Compulsive Disorder   193
    Posttraumatic Stress Disorder   194
    Schizophrenia   195
    Relapse Prevention   196

Starting Points for Help   197

ACKNOWLEDGMENTS

To Linda for all you taught me during your struggle to survive. I regret you lost this battle. I miss you tremendously and will always carry a piece of you in my memories and heart. This book is dedicated to your memory with the hope that it might enlighten those in positions to bring about change and spark hope in those who struggle, as you did, to get through just one more day. You were more special and beautiful than you ever realized. Your kind and gentle spirit touched the lives of many during your short life. I hope you have found the peace you so desperately sought and never found in life.

I extend a genuine thank you from my heart to the hundreds of psychiatric patients I have worked with over the past 10 years at the Houston Veterans Affairs Medical Center. Your willingness to teach me about living with and dying from mental and emotional illness has made me a better therapist and person. I have come to appreciate what it means to have mental health and, for many of you, what it means to struggle with mental illness in a society that emphasizes wellness and upward mobility. Thank you for your courage, tenacity, and insight.

To my husband Vinny who once again silently supports me in my writing endeavors. Thank you for loving me enough to provide the time, patience, and stability I need to complete this project. I know what it costs you and feel sure that God has a special place in heaven reserved for my life partner and best friend. Your presence is the catalyst for all I have accomplished since you came into my life.

PREFACE

This book provides an intimate account of the desperate disguises worn by individuals struggling to live with mental and emotional illness. Their suffering is profound. They long to be "normal" and chase this elusive state of being with all their hearts, often with tragic results. Their struggle merely to survive is made worse by society's unwillingness to validate that mental and emotional illnesses are real and life threatening! I invite you to open your minds and hearts and truly listen to the message this book imparts: our need to acknowledge and take action against this deadly group of illnesses that destroys thousands and leaves a path of emotional destruction in its wake. If you have a mental or emotional illness, I hope something in this book gives you the courage to keep on living. If you live with or love someone with a mental illness, *get involved!* It's not going to "magically disappear" if you ignore it. Get into treatment with your loved one. Help them and help yourself by developing the skills needed to cope with symptoms created by mental and emotional illnesses. If you are a mental health professional *fight* for your clients! Educate others, dispel myths, advocate for political change, provide family education workshops, skills training, resource mobilization, and whatever else it takes to help this special group of people create a life they can live with and enjoy. I hope this book touches you deeply, even moves you to tears. I write it as a wake-up call for us all. This book is about real people with real lives and real suffering. It could be you, me, or someone we love, like my sister Linda. See what you can learn from this book then go out and teach others. The only way things will ever change is if *each* of us takes personal responsibility for making it happen! I have assumed personal responsibility by providing services to the mentally ill and their families, presenting workshops to enlighten the public, and by writing this book. What will *your* role be in this process of education and change?

Part I

Beliefs Create Reality

CHAPTER 1

SOCIAL ATTITUDES: THE SILENT KILLER

It was graduation day. I had waited six long years for this yet I felt woefully unprepared for the job I had accepted and would begin only three short days after receiving my master's degree in social work. I guess the most amazing thing to me was how I could walk up the stairs on the right side of the stage, shake hands with the dean in the center, walk down the stairs on the left side of the stage, and be a professional social worker! Yes, I had studied hard, done two year-long internships, and read enough books to fill a library, but I remembered all too clearly how I had thought I "knew it all" when I was a child and bought my first horse. I had ridden and cared for friends' horses, read books, written off to all kinds of places collecting information on every breed of horse imaginable. Well, when I got that first horse boy did I have a lot to learn! I got kicked, thrown, bumped, banged, and finally, after many episodes of baptism by fire, learned what I *really* needed to know about horses. I had an uneasy feeling social work would also require a number of starts and stops before I felt like a professional.

My first job was on a locked, acute care psychiatry unit at the Houston Veterans Affairs Medical Center. This unit was designed to provide care to mentally ill individuals who were so sick that they required round the clock care on a secured unit to prevent them from wandering into harm's way. I tossed and turned the night before my first day at work. I conjured

3

up all sorts of images of "the mentally ill" and they were very disturbing. I imagined people lurching down the halls, leering, slobbering, laughing hysterically, and talking all sorts of gibberish to themselves and anyone else who cared to listen. I worried about being "locked in" with these dangerous, unpredictable men and women: Would they attack me? Since I was new and very scared, would they, like animals, smell my fear and stalk me since I was an easy target? Even though I was a "professional social worker," I had never really been exposed to mental illness (not at least to *my* way of thinking). My sister, who suffered from depression and a substance abuse disorder, did not seem to fit in this category of people so I never thought of her as mentally ill. After all, weren't mentally ill people really crazy and dangerous? I mean, a person with a *real* mental illness would be locked up in some psych ward, right?

Well, after a night of fitful imaginings and no sleep I reported to duty at the Veterans Affairs hospital. I went through the usual bureaucratic inprocessing and about midmorning was escorted to Ward 312. This ward was secured by two sets of steel doors. I walked through the first set of locked doors and was in a corridor with offices on both sides. My office was to the left. I asked my escort why there were two sets of locked doors (the doors were so sturdy I couldn't imagine why more than one set was needed). I was told, "Oh, that's in case a patient tries to escape. If they manage to get past the first set of doors as someone is coming or going, the nurses can usually catch them before they get through the second set." That raised my anxiety even higher. I was beginning to wonder if I could work in such a dangerous and foreign place.

After putting my belongings in my office, I was escorted through the second set of locked doors onto THE UNIT. I was so anxious I don't think I even noticed the patients. I was too busy worrying about whether I would get out alive. I attended my first staff meeting and was introduced as the new social worker. I sat very apprehensively, on the verge of a panic attack throughout the meeting. At the end of the meeting I walked very stiffly out of the staffing room, down the hall, through the first set of locked doors, and into my office. Then I fell apart. Crying and shaking I thought to myself, "I can't work here! What was I thinking! I'd rather starve to death than go back in there!" The psychologist on the unit had an adjoining office and came in to see why I was crying. She was very supportive and told me that many people had the same reaction and assured me it was not as bad as I thought. She encouraged me to stick around for a few weeks before I decided whether or not to stay. I called my boss who said, "You'll be just fine, it takes some time to get used to the locked units." He loaned me his teddy bear and encouraged me to stick with the job and give myself a chance. He also said, "Once you get to know your patients, you will be surprised what they can teach you. They are wonderful people if you can just get past your own fears and see them for who they really are."

I took his advice and stayed. Looking back 10 years to that first day on the locked unit, I realize how distorted my beliefs were about mental illness. The fact that I was a mental health professional did not dissolve my own distorted views of mental illness. Only after working with this special group of people for 2 years did I really begin to understand the terrible disadvantages they faced, not because they were ill but because of social attitudes about mental illness. I discovered that the general attitude of society is that those wearing the label "mentally ill" were undesirable at best and dangerous at worst. My determination to help others see mental illness as it really is prompted me to write this book.

In this chapter I want to take a look at social attitudes about mental illness. My hope is to share with you what my mentally ill clients taught me; what it is like to face the terrible stigma of being mentally ill in a society that values health and upward mobility above all else. Let's begin by taking a look at *your* beliefs about mental illness. Take a few minutes and write down all the thoughts you have about the term *mentally ill*. Who are

these people, what do they *look* like, how do they act, where
do they live?

_____

_____

_____

_____

_____

Once a month in my clinic I teach a workshop on the myths
and facts about mental illness and these are some of the responses I get:

> The mentally ill are crazy psycho-killers who should be locked
> up forever.
> They are an embarrassment to society and should be hidden away.
> They isolate themselves because they don't really want to be a part
> of society.
> They aren't very smart people.
> People with mental illness are being punished by God.
> People with mental illnesses are not like the rest of us.
> I don't think it really exists; I think people just say they have mental
> problems to get out of working.

Where do these ideas come from? Start by reviewing the
fears and imaginings I shared with you about my early experiences in working with mentally ill patients. Like most of you, I
had never been exposed to "real people" who had mental
illness (remember that for a long time I denied my own sister's
mental illness because she did not fit the stereotype of mental
illness I had created in my mind). Think about some of the
movies you have seen: *One Flew Over the Cuckoos Nest, The Shin-
ing,* and *Psycho.* These movies project images of murder and
mayhem committed by deranged psycho-killers. Social attitudes
stemming from these inaccurate portraits of mental illness
serve only to fuel prejudice and fear. In recent years, movie
makers, pressured by special interest groups, have produced

movies that more accurately depict mental illness, but we have a long way to go! Despite the famous celebrities who have stepped forward and identified themselves as mentally ill, despite the Americans with Disabilities Act, despite recent reforms in mental health care policy, our ability to identify, treat, and include mentally ill individuals in mainstream America is painfully inadequate.

Let's look at each of the above statements and apply them to real people and situations. You will be very surprised at the discrepancy between beliefs and reality—*if* you keep an open mind; I sure was.

STATEMENT 1: "THE MENTALLY ILL ARE CRAZY PSYCHO-KILLERS WHO SHOULD BE LOCKED AWAY FOREVER"

During the past 10 years I've worked in the mental health field, I have worked on locked, acute care units, in day hospital settings, and in outpatient clinics. I have treated clients with diagnoses of schizophrenia, major depression, bipolar disorder (manic-depression), substance abuse and dependence, posttraumatic stress disorder, a number of different personality disorders—I could go on for another paragraph. My experience with individuals in all categories of mental illness is that only a fraction of them ever become violent, and only then when they feel threatened. So why do we have this idea that mentally ill people are deranged psycho-killers? Again, look to the media and how news is reported: "Vietnam veteran with posttraumatic stress disorder goes beserk killing his family and then himself"; "Psychotic killer murders innocent people in a fit of rage"; "Manic-depressive man explodes in restaurant and kills three before being killed by the police"; "Woman with multiple personalities kills husband and children and pleads insanity." These dramatic headlines produce the illusion that mentally ill people are dangerous and should be locked away from others "for the good of society."

I have treated thousands of mentally ill patients over the years. Only one, a man who dropped out of treatment and refused to take medication to control his symptoms, committed a murder-suicide. This patient had a history of violence that predated the onset of his mental illness and I genuinely believe he would have committed this tragic act even in the absence of mental illness. Unfortunately, the media played up his violent act as the direct consequence of mental illness, further supporting the belief that mentally ill people are crazed psycho-killers.

I have seen patients become agitated and upset when psychotic, scream at others, hit walls, and destroy personal effects, but even the sickest generally manage to avoid becoming physically violent unless provoked to the point where *most* of us would become violent! Mr. A is a good example.

Mr. A has a diagnosis of paranoid schizophrenia, which means he hears voices the rest of us do not and these voices tell him that others are out to get him. He was hospitalized many times during my 2 years on Ward 312. Each time he was admitted, it was my job to identify what led to his admission and develop strategies to ease his postdischarge transition back to the community. Mr. A was always very agitated and withdrawn when admitted. He would curl up in his bed, pull the covers over his head, and beg people to leave him alone. After being on medication for a few days, his paranoid thoughts would subside and he would become less agitated and more friendly with staff. At the end of one admission, I said: "Mr. A, each time you come in I have to ask questions and it really upsets you. How can I make the early days of your admission less painful?" He responded: "Jo, when I first come in I am in agony. The voices torture me and I can't think straight enough to answer your questions. If you could just wait a day or two I'll let you know when I can handle the questions." From that day forward I honored his request. He never failed to alert me when he was capable of talking to me. What I learned from Mr. A is that *everyone* has personal boundaries—this is not just true when applied to mental patients! Any one of us, if backed into a corner, has the potential to become defensive or aggressive.

STATEMENT 2: "THEY ARE AN EMBARRASSMENT TO SOCIETY AND SHOULD BE HIDDEN AWAY FOREVER"

Well, folks, we tried this approach in the past and it was disastrous! Locking away individuals with mental illness, or any illness for that matter, does not make the problem go away. Indeed, it compounds the problem by feeding social ignorance, prejudice, and discrimination. When something makes us uncomfortable, a natural reaction is to move away from it. Let me give you an example so you can better understand my reasoning.

My youngest son was born at 27 weeks and as a result of the care required to keep him alive, has visual and hearing impairments. He wears contact lenses and hearing aids. The contacts are invisible so "nobody knows." The hearing aids, on the other hand, are *very* visible! Many people are uncomfortable with my son's disabilities and either ignore us, ask silly questions like, "Why does he wear hearing aids," or chatter aimlessly to relieve their own sense of discomfort. Think about *your own* reactions. How do you act when you see a blind person—many people yell at them thinking they can't hear. How about when you see someone in a wheelchair, you're just not quite sure what to say or do. I'm as guilty as the rest of you, and the only way to overcome this discomfort, be it toward physical or mental disabilities, is to *confront* it!

My own lesson came from a quadriplegic social work student who wanted to complete a training rotation on my service. This was several years before my son was born and I was very apprehensive due to my extreme discomfort with and fear of becoming physically disabled. I agreed to supervise him after telling my fears and asking for his guidance. He told me: "Jo, you know some people see me as handicapped, but I have learned in my 17 years as a quadriplegic that the biggest handicap any of us has is in our own minds." This student taught me a valuable lesson: how to see people for who they really are. This made me a better social worker, and a better mother. I have learned to look at my son, as I do my clients, as a unique and valuable individual. It is my sincere hope that as a society we can all learn to stop handicapping others who look or act differently from the "norm," with our fears, discomfort, and imaginings.

STATEMENT 3: "THEY ISOLATE THEMSELVES BECAUSE THEY DON'T REALLY WANT TO BE A PART OF SOCIETY"

Now, does this really sound like it holds water! Human beings, like many other mammals, are pack animals. This means we crave interaction with others of our own kind. Research has proven that a lack of emotional nurturing in infancy can create a life-threatening condition called "failure to thrive syndrome." Children suffering from this condition are so starved for human contact that they often die even when provided with adequate nutrition. Adult humans are no different! So why, then, do individuals with mental illness shy away from the human contact so desperately needed for survival? Let's look at an example.

Ms. B is a patient who has a mental illness called agoraphobia—a fear of open spaces. Every time Ms. B tries to go out in public, she has panic attacks and feels as if she is dying. Her heart pounds, her throat feels as if it's closing, she experiences dizziness, and becomes so terrified that the only way to relieve the symptoms is to retreat into her apartment. Her mental disorder has progressed to the point where she is at risk of dying because she can no longer force herself to go out to handle even the most basic tasks: buying food, doing laundry, paying bills. Day after day she sits in her apartment, alone and afraid. If she attempts to go out, she risks activating her fear of dying or going crazy. If she sits at home, she risks death from malnutrition and social isolation. It certainly doesn't sound as though Ms. B "likes" to be alone, or that she avoids social contact because she doesn't *want* to be part of society, does it?

There are a number of mental illnesses that place patients in the double bind of being forced into isolation to avoid activating symptoms of their illness. An analogy might help you make this connection. Picture a dog who has been so badly abused it is afraid to approach a plate of food for fear of being beaten again. In some cases, the fear is so intense, the animal will starve to death rather than risk another beating, even when there is no visible source of threat. Humans are no different. Repeated negative experiences "teach" us to avoid potential sources of pain at all costs, even when to do so jeopardizes our safety and well-being. Let's look at another example.

Mr. C suffers from posttraumatic stress disorder (PTSD). He fought in the Korean War and every day he spent there he was at risk of dying. The incident that forever changed his life was being surrounded by enemy troops and watching as his fellow soldiers were picked off one at a time. He survived because enemy troops, noting the severity of his wounds, left him for dead. This veteran, some 40 years later, continues to reexperience this event in nightmares and thoughts about the war that come on suddenly, without provocation. He has difficulty sleeping, jumps when he hears loud noises, has difficulty being around others, and feels emotionally "dead" inside. Although he desperately longs to be with others, memories of the tremendous losses in his past keep him from reaching out. This is compounded by his intense anxiety. One minute he feels fine, but the next minute he is overcome with fear or confusion. He finds this inability to control his emotions very embarrassing so he has resigned himself to a lonely and unhappy life—the price for being a combat survivor. It doesn't sound as though he enjoys being socially isolated any more than Ms. B, does it?

STATEMENT 4: "THEY AREN'T VERY SMART PEOPLE"

This statement makes about as much sense as calling a deaf person dumb! Just because they can't hear doesn't mean they can't think! Likewise, mental illness does not imply mental retardation. Most individuals with mental illnesses have average or above average I.Q.'s. Many such people have lived highly productive lives before their disease became active. I have worked with former doctors, lawyers, psychologists, social workers, housewives, pilots, engineers, and machinists. Many are educated, most are motivated to be productive, and all are painfully aware of their losses. To label them stupid is yet another blow to their already tattered self-esteem. Mentally *ill* does *not* mean mentally *retarded* any more that schizophrenia means multiple personalities. Each is a distinct condition which merits being identified and treated as such. What you don't know *can* hurt you and others—please take the time to learn about a particular disorder or condition before you go around spreading misinformation. Ignorance is the root of prejudice; stamp it out before it gets a foothold.

STATEMENT 5: "PEOPLE WITH MENTAL ILLNESSES ARE BEING PUNISHED BY GOD"

Mixing religion and mental health is a dangerous thing, much like mixing bleach and ammonia: Alone they are relatively harmless if you follow instructions, but when mixed together they create toxic fumes. Mental illness is no more the result of God's wrath than is AIDS, cancer, or any other human ailment. They are diseases not moral judgments against evil human beings. I know many of you would argue differently, but if mental illness is a penance for bad behavior, why then does it strike children, and those who have only done good in their lives? My sister is a good example.

Linda was a kind, gentle person who never intentionally

harmed another human being. She was so sensitive as a child, my mother said she would cry at the mildest hint of a scolding. She was a good student, a good wife, and a good mother. She was the kind of daughter who always remembered Mother's Day; the granddaughter who spent countless hours listening to grandma's stories about days gone by. She was a hospice volunteer, a volunteer who taped books for the blind, she was a scout leader, a person who took children to sing in nursing homes at Christmas. Does this sound like a person God would punish to the point that led her to say, "Jo, my life is like being trapped in the pages of a bad book and I can't get out!" I think not. Linda suffered from a major mental illness called depression and a second called addiction. One fed the other and they slowly leeched away the person she once was leaving a shell filled with agony and pain. In my heart I cannot imagine a God of any religion initiating such a calculated course of destruction on one who had never deliberately harmed another. I hope this story makes you think when you find yourself passing moralistic judgments on others. Nobody asks for or deserves mental illness. The term *mental illness* defines a broad category of diseases that randomly strikes those with genetic, physical, metabolic, emotional, personality, and social vulnerabilities. It attacks with such swiftness that there is often no warning and never an escape. It is real and life threatening. Take it seriously for what it is, not for what you imagine it to be.

STATEMENT 6: "PEOPLE WITH MENTAL ILLNESSES ARE NOT LIKE THE REST OF US"

My rhetorical question in response to this statement is always, "What are the rest of us like?" I invite my workshop participants, as I now invite you, to provide descriptions for people who are *not* mentally ill. Some of the answers I have received include:

They have jobs and are responsible for their families.

They set goals for the future.
They have friends and social interests.
They want to make life better for themselves and their children.
They care about themselves and others.
They are interested in world events and the environment.
They have hopes, dreams, and ambitions for the future.

After I write these responses on the board, we compare them to the myths of mental illness (statements 1–7 that we are currently exploring). The startling revelation for most participants, and I hope for you as well, is that individuals who are mentally ill *really* want the same things, but the symptoms of their respective illnesses often prevent them from achieving these goals. Most want to work and feel like productive members of society, they long for friends and social connections, care deeply about their families, are interested in the world, and have as many hopes and dreams as their healthy counterparts.

If people with mental illnesses have the same hopes, dreams, needs, and desires that people without mental illnesses have, why do we label them "different"? Simple, if we see them for the real flesh-and-blood people they are instead of the crazed psycho-killer weirdos we imagine them to be, we will begin to *feel* their pain. A combat veteran helped me understand this by relating a story about behavior on the battlefield. He told me that in the Vietnam War, one form of psychological warfare was to mutilate enemy bodies since Vietnamese people believe a mutilated body cannot enter heaven. American soldiers often cut off ears, fingers, and other body parts of dead and dying enemy soldiers to psychologically terrorize enemy troops. He said they also took money and other possessions as trophies, but always destroyed personal items such as pictures. When asked why, he responded: "You didn't want to think of them as human, as having parents, wives, and kids. Once you started seeing them as human it made killing so much harder. The only way to survive was to reduce the enemy to a subhuman status. Then you could rationalize that you are killing the enemy not someone's son, husband, father." The same philosophy applies to mental illness. If we reduce this group of people to a subhuman status by labeling them "not like the rest of us," we can avoid dealing with their pain and suffering. After all, they are not like us so why should we care? Indeed, how can we not care since each of these individuals *is* somebody's child, spouse, parent, friend?

STATEMENT 7: "I DON'T THINK IT REALLY EXISTS; I THINK PEOPLE JUST SAY THEY HAVE MENTAL PROBLEMS TO GET OUT OF WORKING"

We will explore this issue in great detail in another chapter, so suffice it to say that since most people with mental illnesses "look" just like the rest of us, it's hard to believe they are really ill. If I see someone with a missing arm or leg, with hearing aids or a seeing eye dog, if I see a person with a disfigured face from cancer surgery or scars indicating they were once badly burned, I almost always feel empathy or can at least rationalize their need for a little extra help from society. What about those with "invisible illnesses"? There are people with anxiety disorders who have immobilizing panic attacks, or those who suffer from depression so profound that it takes every ounce of energy they have just to get out of bed. How about the person with schizophrenia who cannot determine whether the voices they hear are real or only the imaginings of their own minds? What about the combat veteran with posttraumatic stress disorder? He certainly *looks* healthy so why does he "freak out" when he has to be around other people or do a structured job that creates a little stress? I have to deal with the stress of working and daily life, if I can do it, why can't he?

This line of thinking creates major handicaps for those with mental illnesses. They beat themselves up for being unable to participate in mainstream society, and just when they are about to make the adjustment to being disabled, someone accuses them of being lazy or just not trying hard enough. Even those who try to hide their illnesses and continue working face discrimination and the risk of rejection. Let's look at a common example.

I apply for a job. If I tell the prospective employer I have a mental condition and take psychotropic medications to manage my symptoms I may not get hired. If I intentionally leave this information out, I will most likely get fired if they later discover this fact. I know, I can hear you saying, "But that's illegal! What about the Americans with Disabilities Act?" Well, ideal and real often fail to line up on the same page. Take my client Mr. Y, he is a locomotive engineer. Although he would benefit greatly from medication to reduce symptoms of depression, he is fearful of being fired. His company has a policy by which they review such issues on a "case by case basis." Although the company cannot legally fire Mr. Y if he can perform his duties and a psychiatrist clears him to continue employment as an engineer, even while medicated, the company can always find other "legitimate" reasons to fire him so as not to upset the apple cart. The fear of losing employment forces my client to suffer unnecessarily. When are we, as a society, going to become more progressive in our view of mental illness, psychiatric treatment, and medication for long-term symptom management? After all, we don't blink an eye when someone tells us they take medication for high blood pressure, diabetes, or a thyroid condition. These medications help them manage symptoms so they can remain "productive members of society." Well, psychotropic medications used to treat symptoms of mental illness are designed for the same reason: to allow individuals to reach their highest level of functioning and live lives as normal as possible.

One final example will demonstrate the tremendous frustration faced by those with mental illnesses who simply cannot work no matter how hard they try. Again, it is a story from my sister's life. My sister struggled to work for a number of years.

Working stressed her beyond safe limits, yet in the interest of her family, she continued to "put her best foot forward." She felt very strongly about her financial contributions to her family. After multiple hospitalizations and several serious suicide attempts, she finally acknowledged that no matter how much she wanted to work, she simply could not hold herself together enough to successfully maintain employment. This realization led her to apply for Social Security Disability Insurance (SSDI) so she could continue to contribute to the family's economic well-being. This federally funded insurance program is set up out of taxpayer dollars to fund those of us who have paid into Social Security and who, for whatever reason, become unable to work for a period expected to last at least 2 years. The application process is long and tedious. A rejected claim the first time around is almost guaranteed. My sister, like most of my clients, faced the stressful task of assembling medical records to support her claim. She suffered embarrassment and frustration when processing clerks treated her "as if" she were really not ill. She did finally receive SSDI benefits. Her appeal was approved *after* her death. I have no way of knowing whether or not the stigma and humiliation of fighting for benefits she was entitled to hastened her death, but as I watch hundreds of my clients go through this demeaning process, I cannot help but believe that it contributes to their downward spiraling sense of worthlessness.

The above statements are but a sample of the negative stereotypes faced by those among us who suffer from mental illness. I hope this chapter has provided a fresh perspective, a less biased opinion, or at least food for thought when you think about the term *mental illness*. In the following chapter we will take a closer look at mental illness and the people behind the labels.

Chapter 2

Understanding Mental Illness

In chapter 1 we explored what mental illness is *not*. This chapter will take a closer look at what mental illness *is*, and who it affects, and will then present anecdotes to show how very much mentally ill individuals are "like the rest of us." Let's begin by exploring the term *mental illness*. This term encompasses hundreds of disorders as defined in the *Diagnostic and Statistical Manual of Mental Disorders* (DSM-IV; APA, 1994). This 875-page book is a tool used by mental health professionals to assign appropriate diagnoses to patients' presenting problems. The DSM-IV identifies 16 major categories of mental illnesses:

- Delirium, dementia, and amnesiac and other disorders
- Mental disorders due to medical conditions
- Substance abuse disorders
- Schizophrenia and other psychotic disorders
- Mood disorders
- Anxiety disorders
- Somatoform disorders
- Factitious disorders
- Dissociative disorders
- Sexual and gender identity disorders
- Eating disorders
- Sleep disorders
- Impulse control disorders
- Adjustment disorders
- Personality disorders

• Other conditions that may be a focus of clinical attention

I will not discuss these categories or the hundreds of mental and emotional disorders identified under each category due to the nature of this book. My sole purpose of identifying them is to demonstrate the extensive number of conditions that qualify as mental and emotional disorders. As we learned in the first chapter, most individuals with mental and emotional disorders walk among us undetected. Looking at the categories above, you can see why. Many mental problems can be carefully masked from the world's view and only become apparent to those with whom the affected individual lives. "Well," I hear you thinking, "if that's the case what's the big deal about mental illness? Why do we need to identify and treat it more effectively if so many people get by fine just the way things are?" Some statistics from the National Mental Health Association will help answer this question.

• More than 51 million Americans have a mental disorder in a single year (NIMH and CMHS, 1994).
• During the course of any given year, while more than 40 million adult Americans are affected by one or more mental disorders, 5.5 million Americans are disabled by severe mental illness (NIMH, 1990).
• Preliminary studies indicate that 1 in 5 children/adolescents (20%) may have a diagnosable disorder. Estimates of the number of children who have mental disorders range from 7.7 million to 12.8 million (CMHS, 1993). These young people are estimated to have severe emotional or behavioral problems that significantly interfere with their daily functioning.
• Less than one-third of the children under age 18 with a serious emotional disturbance receive mental health services. Often, the services are inappropriate (Children's Defense Fund) (CMHS-Mental Health, U.S., 1994).
• An estimated 19.9 million Americans (8.8% of the population) experience phobias. About 9.1 million (5.1%) live with major depression. Some 3.9 million have obsessive compulsive disorder; 2 million experience bipolar disorders (Mental Health, U.S., 1994; NMHA, 1993).

- At least two-thirds of elderly nursing home residents have a diagnosis of a mental disorder such as major depression (NIMH, 1990)
- Up to 25% of the population with AIDS will develop AIDS-related cognitive dysfunction. Two-thirds of all people with AIDS will develop neuropsychiatric problems (Mental Health Liaison Group, 1993).
- A majority of the 29,000 Americans who commit suicide each year are believed to have a mental disorder. Suicide is the eighth leading cause of death in the United States and the third leading cause of death among people aged 15 to 24 (NIMH, 1994).
- Nearly one-third of the nation's estimated 600,000 homeless individuals are believed to be severely mentally ill adults (CMHS, 1992).
- More than 1 in 14 jail inmates has a mental illness. Twenty-nine percent of the nation's jails routinely hold people with mental illnesses without any criminal charges (National Alliance for the Mentally Ill and Public Citizens Health Research Group, 1992).

I feel these statistics are very significant, and indeed, demand inclusion here. By now it should be apparent that the term *mental illness* is a very broad umbrella under which hundreds of mental and emotional disorders exist. The statistics from the National Mental Health Association speak further of the widespread nature of mental and emotional illnesses and the devastating consequences to individuals, families, and society (we'll look further at this issue in chapter 10). I hope this brief overview has heightened your awareness regarding the seriousness of this national health issue.

ASSIGNING A LABEL

Let's move on to explore some of the concepts that apply to mental illness and how they influence individuals' prognosis

Source: The above statistics are from the Mental Health Information Center, National Mental Health Association, Alexandria, Virginia. For further information on these statistics, contact: Office of External Liaison, Center for Mental Health Services, 5600 Fishers Lane, Room 13-103, Rockville, Maryland 20857; telephone (301) 443-2792.

(anticipated outcome). The first concept of importance is the whole idea of *assigning a label* of "mental illness" to an individual. As we saw in chapter 1, this label often creates a social stigma that severely limits an individual's ability to secure work, maintain relationships, and participate fully in society. Why, then, do we label? The single most important reason is so that when mental health professionals (psychiatrists, psychologists, social workers, nurses, or counselors to name a few) review a patient's chart and read the diagnoses they immediately understand the nature of the patient's symptoms, and recommended treatment modalities.

Let's look at a few examples. A diagnosis of major depression, recurrent, with melancholia tells me this individual has experienced symptoms including sadness, a sense of hopelessness, changes in sleep and appetite, a change in his or her normal level of social interaction, loss of energy, loss of pleasure in usual activities, and so on. It also tells me this has happened before (it's recurring) and that the individual's symptoms are worse in the morning (with melancholia). A diagnosis of antisocial personality disorder tells me this individual has experienced problems that stem back to childhood in relating to others and the rules of society. It also tells me this person has a history of committing acts which have broken social norms, violated laws, or harmed others, and that they have little or no remorse for these actions. This is important information so I will know what types of treatment to use and the individual's potential for a productive life after treatment. As you can see, labeling, despite the risk of stigma, is vital to effective mental health interventions.

THE ISSUE OF INTENSITY

A second concept of importance is *the issue of intensity*. Simply stated, this means how badly is the individual affected by his or her symptoms. On a scale from not at all to severe impairment in functioning, I know whether this individual is currently able to function fairly well and needs only minor intervention or if their condition is so severe that hospitalization is needed to protect them until their symptoms can be stabilized. People often look at the label an individual wears instead of the intensity of symptoms, and this does a true disservice to the patient. I have worked with some very high functioning individuals with schizophrenia who were able to maintain themselves independently and get through daily life basically unsupervised. Likewise, I have known patients with antisocial personality disorders so severe that they were unable to work, maintain relationships, and felt so hopeless about their situation they wanted to die. An analogy is to compare the I.Q. points of a individual who is severely retarded with someone who is gifted. It just isn't fair to expect the same performance from each individual since their abilities and limitations differ markedly. The moral: Don't judge a person by their label—you may end up doing more harm than good. This becomes especially important in family relationships which we will discuss in depth in chapter 10.

THE ISSUE OF DURATION

A third concept of importance is *the issue of duration*. Duration means how long the person has been affected with their mental illness (i.e., is it acute—did it just happen, or chronic—has it been there for a long time). In general, the longer a condition is present, the higher the number of negative symptoms the individual will experience. A good example is the difference in an acute stress reaction and posttraumatic stress disorder (PTSD). If a firefighter attempts to save the life of a badly injured child and the child dies, he or she is likely to experience an acute stress reaction (feel anxious). Immediate intervention, designed to help this firefighter put the event in perspective, can prevent this reaction from developing into the more chronic condition posttraumatic stress disorder (PTSD). Symptoms commonly experienced by individuals affected with PTSD include anxiety, intrusive thoughts about the event, night-mares, flashbacks, feelings of detachment, emotional numb-ness, avoidance of things that remind them of the traumatic event, sleep disturbances, irritability or anger outbursts, poor concentration, and a tendency to startle easily. These symptoms disable individuals so profoundly they are unable to sustain employment, friendships, or family relationships. Think of a more common issue. If I break my foot and immediately have the bone set, I have a good chance of complete recovery. If, however, treatment is delayed, I might get a bone infection, or have other complications that prevent my foot from fully recovering. Another example is a woman who discovers a breast lump. If she immediately seeks help, she may only need a lum-pectomy, meaning she not only preserves her life but also most of her breast. If, however, she puts off treatment, if she has cancer it may spread so she loses her entire breast, or worse, her life.

THE ISSUE OF SINGLE OR RECURRENT SYMPTOMS

A fourth concept of importance is the issue of *single* or *recur-rent.* Simply stated, did the person only experience the symp-toms one time or do the symptoms keep coming back over and over again? In general, the person who has a single episode has a better chance of full recovery than does their counterpart with recurring symptoms. Let's take the diagnosis of major de-pression as an example. If the depression is related to a specific event (death of a loved one, divorce, major life change) the chance of recurrence is small and most people make a full recovery. If, however, the depression is endogenous (meaning stemming from a genetic predisposition and biochemical im-balance in the brain) the individual has a much higher risk of recurring episodes. The issue of single versus recurring plays a big role in the intensity and duration of symptoms discussed above. The more often episodes of illness occur, the more in-tense and severe will be the symptoms.

SINGLE VS. DUAL DIAGNOSIS

Finally, the concept of *single* versus *dual diagnosis* plays an important role in an individual's long-term prognosis. A simple analogy is juggling. I can easily juggle one apple, maybe even two without many mistakes. If another two to three apples are added, my risk of dropping one or all of them greatly increases. Likewise, if I have more than one mental illness, the likelihood that the symptoms of one will increase symptoms of another increases. Most of the clients I treat have PTSD. Many also have substance abuse disorders. If they try to stay sober, negative memories of their trauma surface which greatly increases their risk of relapse. If they try to do trauma work before achieving sobriety, they may be unable to get in touch with underlying emotional reactions which it is vital that they identify and resolve so they can move beyond their trauma. In treating dually diagnosed clients, the trick is not which came first (because each disorder is a distinct condition that merits treatment) but rather, which should be treated first to increase the likelihood of a successful outcome (i.e., higher life satisfaction).

The above information is basically all you will ever need as a mental health consumer (i.e., patient with one or more mental illnesses, a family member, or a friend). The goal has been to increase your awareness of this very complicated issue and to provide a starting point for a better understanding of mental illness. The final goal of this chapter is, through the use of anecdotes, to give you a closer look at the people behind the label "mental illness." They are warm, intelligent, loving, and surprisingly insightful. Please join me in this journey back to some of my most interesting encounters as a mental health professional.

THE HARDWARE MAN

Mr. D was one of the first patients I treated 10 years ago as the new social worker on Ward 312. He was diagnosed with chronic

paranoid schizophrenia and had been hospitalized more than
20 times over the years of his illness. He seldom took his
medication because the side-effects it created were often more
disturbing that the symptoms of his illness. Psychiatric
medications can produce a number of unpleasant side-effects
including sleep disturbances, sexual impotence, weight gain or
loss, dry mouth, nausea, confusion, blunted affect, and, in some
cases, a more serious condition know as tardive dyskenesia.
Symptoms of this condition can range from barely noticeable
such as involuntary blinking, lip-licking, tongue-twitching, or
foot-tapping to more startling symptoms like writhing, rocking,
twisting, jerking, flexing and stiffening any or all parts of the
body. Because Mr. D's symptoms were severe, he stopped taking
his medication each time he was discharged from the hospital.
As a result, he quickly became psychotic and the voices in his
head gave him all sorts of disturbing messages. This patient
had experienced his first psychotic break at age 19 while on
active duty in the army. Since it was service related, he drew a
compensation check of $1,600 monthly. Despite this income,
he lived in the streets and ate out of garbage cans. The most
peculiar thing Mr. D did when psychotic was to visit hardware
stores and eat nuts, bolts, and nails until someone caught him
and chased him out of the store. This generally led to medical
problems, which was the case just before I met him. He had
been hospitalized on a surgical ward to have the latest round
of hardware removed, then transferred to psychiatry for observation and treatment. He had multiple scars from surgeries to
remove foreign objects. When I asked why he ate hardware, he
responded, "Because the voices tell me if I eat enough metal
I will become impervious to pain."

Well, as a new social worker I was absolutely horrified! I
took it as my personal responsibility to "save" this poor schizophrenic. I spent hours researching housing options, sheltered
day programs, guardians to help him manage his funds. When
his discharge day arrived, I met with him to finalize his plans.
I had picked "the perfect" living arrangement and was ready

to activate many other referrals that *I* thought would be good for him. He was very attentive as I described all these plans, then looked at me and said, "Jo, I know you are new at this and trying to help, but you don't understand. I would much rather live in the streets and eat garbage than in a halfway house were I have no privacy and others dictate my daily activities." At this response I became so concerned a tear slipped silently down my cheek. I said, "Mr. D, if you keep living this way, eating hardware and wandering the streets, you'll die." He gently wiped the tear from my face and responded, "Jo, I have to live my life as best I can. It makes me feel good to know someone cares, but you can't choose what's best for anyone but yourself." In the years following this encounter I have come to understand what Mr. D was trying to tell me: That each individual must make what he or she feels is the right choice in purely personal terms, regardless of what others think, and that if I, as a social worker, tried to play God, I would only create misery for all involved. I have often wondered what happened to Mr. D, but I will never forget his patience and gentleness as he struggled to teach me the art of letting the patient be where he or she is.

THE WRONG CHART

Mr. E was also one of my first patients on Ward 312. He was admitted for major depression after becoming so despondent that he had attempted suicide. Part of my job as the social worker was to complete an assessment on admission (to identify any problems of a social nature that might require my attention), and to assist patients with discharge planning (follow-up treatment, housing, finances, and so on). Ward 312 was a very busy unit and on the day I planned to meet with Mr. E to discuss his aftercare plans, I had five other patients who also needed my attention. I had pulled all their charts and had them scattered across the top of my desk. I called Mr. E into

my office and began to review his plans. I said, "Looks like you
have adequate income and will be returning home to your
wife." He responded, "Yeah, I'm luckier than some of the people up here." I then went on to discuss his plans for continuing
psychiatric care and we both agreed he would be followed by
his private psychiatrist since he had been seeing him for about
6 months, liked him, and had the insurance benefits to cover
weekly visits. It appeared all was in order *except* we had not yet
addressed his cardiac problems. The chart indicated Mr. E had
serious heart problems which required regular supervision.
Contentious social worker that I was, I said, "Mr. E, I see you
have a cardiac condition—where do you go for follow-up?" He
looked as though I had bitten him and responded, "What do
you mean I have a cardiac problem, nobody ever told *me* that!"
We were both quite flustered. I glanced at the chart to double
check the diagnosis and realized I was reading from another
patient's record! Of course I was mortified and *knew* I would
be fired immediately (I was only 2 weeks into my job). When I
acknowledged my mistake, Mr. E looked *very* relieved and said,
"Well, honey, I guess we both learned something. You learned
that you need to be more careful about whose chart you're
reading and I learned that I should be grateful that things
aren't any worse than they are!" The psychologist on the unit
later told me that Mr. E had recounted this story in group, and
had said, "I just thought my life was bad until that social worker
told me I had a heart problem. Once she told me she had
made a mistake, I realized how lucky I am." Obviously I didn't
lose my job and this patient's sense of humor and compassion
for the "new kid on the block" helped me get through one of
the most traumatic mistakes of my young career.

THE ANTISOCIAL WITH A HEART

Mr. F was an alcohol dependent client with a severe antisocial
personality disorder. He had a lengthy prison record for assault, aggravated assault, driving while intoxicated, domestic

violence, and robbery. When I met him I was working in the outpatient alcohol treatment program at the Houston Veterans Affairs Medical Center. His sole reason for enrollment was to avoid a long prison sentence following yet another assault charge. His parole officer had given him the ultimatum "make this treatment program work for you or I'll throw away the key when they lock you up this time." His visit with me was to set up a schedule of attendance he could live with and to help him identify resources for housing and basic needs. About half way through the interview my telephone rang. I answered and told my clerk, "I'm with someone, please take a message." She responded "Jo, you *have* to take this call." I reluctantly agreed and the voice on the other end was my mother saying, "Joanne, we found your sister dead this morning, please come home." I was in shock and remember saying to Mr. F, "My sister is dead, I can keep myself together long enough to finish helping you, then I have to go home." There sat one of the most violent antisocial patients I had ever worked with, watching me shake and struggle to keep my emotions under control until I could leave. He had a perfect opportunity to act out, but instead, got very soft and said, "Jo, I can tell you are very upset and my stuff can wait, go ahead and leave now, I'll be O.K." At that point he was much more functional than I was, and I took his advice. Several weeks later he stopped by to reschedule his appointment. He told me how sorry he was that my sister had died and that he hoped I felt better soon. This encounter taught me a lot about people. It taught me not to look at someone's past behavior and diagnosis and automatically assume the worst. Mr. F taught me that in times of crisis, even the most dysfunctional individuals can extend themselves in support of others.

THE COMPASSIONATE ALCOHOLIC

Mr. G was another of my clients in the outpatient alcohol treatment program. He was participating in my anger management/relapse prevention program when my sister died. Of course I canceled all my groups and other staff members simply told my patients that my sister had died and I would be out for the week. Mr. G was a chronic alcoholic with many, many treatment attempts. His struggle to achieve and maintain sobriety was ongoing and his chance of success very small since he had no family, few resources, and many problems. This client rode the bus to the clinic because he was too poor to own a car. This same client read about my sister's funeral arrangements and *walked* from downtown Houston to the East Side of the city (about 15 miles) to extend his sympathies to my family. Although I was very uncomfortable having him see me in crisis, I have never forgotten his compassion and the length he went just to let me know he cared. What Mr. G taught me was that people who have suffered have a special understanding of emotional pain and almost always try to ease the pain of others, even when they cannot ease their own.

The Upbeat Schizophrenic

Mr. H was a man in his early 50's who had suffered with chronic paranoid schizophrenia for most of his adult life. His symptoms were so severe that he required supervised housing and assistance remembering when to take his medication. This patient had a strong desire to be productive and volunteered hundreds of hours at the Veterans Hospital each year. We always knew when Mr. H was getting sick again because he would walk up giggling gibberish and follow you around. When he was well, he was the most upbeat, optimistic person I have ever met. Mr. H always greeted people in the halls, and he had a special word for each day of the week to describe how he was doing. I would say, "Hi Mr. H, how are you today?" He would respond, "What day is it?" I would give the appropriate response and he would then provide the answer. On Mondays he was marvelous, Tuesdays tremendous, Wednesdays wonderful, Thursdays terrific, and Fridays fabulous. I never saw him on the weekends but I'm sure he had upbeat responses for those days of the week too. This patient always made me laugh and taught me that no matter how bad things are, you can *always* find some good in each day and work to make at least a few other people smile. Sadly, Mr. H died this year. When I walk down the halls, I still look for him and really miss his upbeat responses. I guess those of us who knew him will have to keep the tradition of enthusiasm he started alive. He was a very sick man but always took his role at the Veterans Hospital very seriously—he will be missed sorely by us all.

A Card with Love

When my youngest son was born very prematurely it was a long time before we knew whether or not he would survive. At the time I was still working in the outpatient alcohol treatment program but did a weekly addiction education group in the Day Hospital. This treatment setting provided daily care to patients who were sick enough to need daily care but not sick enough to be hospitalized. Most had diagnoses of major depression, bipolar disorder, personality disorders, or anxiety disorders. When my son was born the Day Hospital staff told the patients since I was unable to lead my group for several weeks. One day I received a card in the mail, it was a collective effort from all my patients. Each had written special thoughts or prayers inside the card which the staff then mailed to me. It was filled with such love and concern that I cried. Here were these very sick individuals reaching out to *me* in my time of need. I still see some of these patients and they always ask after my "miracle child." Yet another lesson in the extension of self even in times of distress and dysfunction.

The Diaper Bag

The I's had participated in my family group for about 3 months before my son was born. They were a lively couple struggling to cope with the effects Mr. I's alcoholism was having on their marriage. They made good progress in group, learning to work collectively in attacking symptoms *not* each other. I returned to work after a lengthy maternity leave and found a beautifully wrapped gift on my desk. I opened this gift and inside was the most magnificent diaper bag! It had everything a new mother could ever want. Since we are not allowed to accept gifts, I began asking around so I could find out who to both thank and return the gift to. One of the addiction therapists said, "Jo, the I's brought this gift for you and it is really important to them that you keep it. Bring the diaper bag to team meeting and see what the others say before you return it." I took the diaper bag to our next team meeting and set it dead center on the table saying, "I got this from the I's and know I can't keep it since it's from a patient. Help me think of a way to return it without hurting their feelings." The entire team of 7 looked at me and responded, "What diaper bag?" The lesson I learned from this exchange was that sometimes you have to look at the symbolism of a gift rather than steadfastly enforcing the rules.

THE WALL

When I began working in the Trauma Recovery Program 3 years ago, I had little specialized knowledge about trauma interventions and almost none about the Vietnam War. Many of my patients are Vietnam veterans anywhere from 10 to 15 years older than I. When I attended the "Walk-Through Vietnam" group (a special group to help combat survivors put their traumatic experiences in perspective), one very outspoken veteran said, "Why are *you* in here? *Where the hell were you* when *we* were in Vietnam?" My response: "I was in the 6th grade struggling with training bras and trying to figure out why people were wearing those little metal bracelets that had a name and the letters MIA on them." He accepted this response, so I went on to say, "I'm a pretty good therapist and you guys are experts on the Vietnam War and on being trauma survivors. If we work together I think we can generate some good results for all of us." I didn't think much about it after that. This is a *very* closed group of combat veterans who rarely allow a noncombat veteran much less a nonveteran inside their circle. I respected this boundary and went about trying to provide the best clinical interventions that I could.

One day I attended a psychodrama session. This is a type of therapy that encourages clients to "act out" their trauma in a variety of structured group exercises and role-plays. During this particular session a Navy Seal (special forces combat veteran) passed around a beautifully framed picture of the Vietnam memorial wall with a poem his dead friend had written superimposed on the wall. When the picture came to me, I admired it and was preparing to pass it. He said, "No, Jo, I brought that for *you*. Because you are so honest about what you know and don't know, you've earned it. The word has gotten around, and you're all right even though you are a woman and a nonveteran." This moved me deeply since trust is a major issue for combat veterans with PTSD. This Navy Seal taught me another valuable lesson: That as a therapist, being willing to voice both my strengths and limitations, and respect patients' need for time to develop trust, would reap rich rewards. In this case, the reward was being allowed inside a tightly guarded circle of combat veterans. Their willingness to risk and to trust has made me a more effective helper.

The primary reason why I'm telling all these stories is that I want you to get a taste of the people behind the label "mental illness." The reason I have seen the things I relate in these stories is because I meet my clients where they are, I respect their integrity, I honor their humanity, and I recognize and acknowledge that they are, indeed, "just like the rest of us." Because society in general passes judgment on that which it fails to understand (and yes, it counts even if you don't know any better—when I wrecked my moped in Cozumel because I thought the gas was the brake the end result was that I wrecked the moped! It didn't change the outcome because "I didn't know better). In addition, most of us (and as you saw in chapter 1 I have been as guilty as the rest of you) do not create an atmosphere of acceptance so individuals with mental illnesses can be who they *really* are! The following six chapters will provide a startling account of the desperate disguises worn by those afflicted with mental illnesses in their struggle for survival and acceptance. I hope you will take each chapter seriously and read with an open mind. Chances are that you will see yourself, or someone you love, along the way.

PART II

THE DEADLY MASQUERADE

CHAPTER 3

THE PICTURE OF HEALTH

Peer acceptance and social approval: the keys to success in American society. From early childhood we learn how important it is to "put our best foot forward." Our parents and teachers stress the significance of "first impressions." Friends remind us that being part of the "in crowd" means looking, acting, walking, and talking cool. The phrases "dress for success," "looks are everything," "actions speak louder than words," and "the package sells the product" are constant reminders of how important others' opinions are in shaping our success.

Think back to your own adolescence. Remember how important those weekend outings to the movies or the skating rink were? Friday night: You have plans to meet your friends at the local movie theater. You put on your best jeans, your coolest shirt, and your finest shoes. You carefully style your hair and then, just when you think you're set, you see it: the zit from hell! Although it's actually the size of a pinhead, in your mind this destroyer of coolness is threatening to take over your entire body! You frantically try to cover it up with Clearasil, cover sticks, or whatever else is handy. You make excuses to avoid having to face your friends. If you *do* go, the evening is spent trying to keep everybody from seeing just how gross you look.

As we get older we laugh at how intense we were about every zit, every wrinkle, every misplaced hair—until we meet

37

our true love! Then it starts all over again! We dress to impress, take every care not to pass gas, belch, pick our teeth, noses, or anything else vulgar. We talk nice, act nice, pay attention to *everything* this dream person says (no matter how boring it is). In essence, we paint a picture that we *think* this person wants to see! This is a very stressful process! Thank goodness once we get into intimate relationships with long-term partners, develop friendships where we are accepted for who we are, and work some place long enough to become friendly with our coworkers, we can stop all this nonsense.

Yes, we *all* wear public faces, work hard to preserve our professional images, and pay careful attention to outward appearances. What a relief it is at the end of each day to retreat to our homes and families, our safe haven from the scrutiny of the world, to be *who we really are!* Once behind closed doors we can let down our hair, look frumpy, pass gas, belch, have stinky morning breath, wear holey underwear, say how we really think and feel about ourselves and life in general, and still be loved and accepted for who we are.

What about those among us who have mental or emotional illnesses? The symptoms experienced by people with mental and emotional problems often lead to feelings and thoughts that, if stated out loud, alarm or upset others. Most of my patients are painfully aware of this fact. Even when they are behind closed doors they continue to present "the picture of health" to avoid causing pain or discomfort to others. How comfortable would you be saying to your family or closest friends some of the things my patients dare only to share in therapy:

> I sat in the park last night with a loaded 357 magnum in my mouth trying to decide whether or not to pull the trigger.
> The voices are back, they keep telling me I can escape the pain by killing myself.
> I keep having nightmares about the people I killed in combat. I still see their faces. I can still hear them screaming.

I never feel real unless I hurt myself. When I hurt myself it reminds me that I *must* be real or I wouldn't feel pain.

I never feel normal if I'm not drunk or high. It's just too scary to think about stopping.

If my family or friends ever knew what I *really* feel, they would be horrified! I don't want to hurt them any more than I already have so it's best to keep this stuff inside.

I've been wearing this mask for so long, I'm scared to take it off even when I'm alone. I'm afraid of what I might see.

I have so much anger inside I feel like a time bomb ready to explode.

My life is like looking at the sun without sunglasses on and I can't turn away.

I save up pills to kill myself then I realize how wrong this is. I flush them down the toilet then immediately panic! I have to start saving them up again to keep myself from freaking out. Just knowing death is an option helps me keep from totally losing it.

I used to love having company but now whenever someone comes over I have to wipe all the fingerprints off everything they touch or they will die of a heart attack. It's so stressful having to watch their every move without them noticing. I have to though because if I miss even one object, they will be doomed and it will be my fault.

Everyone I get close to dies or leaves. My family doesn't understand why I stay so emotionally distant and I can't tell them because they wouldn't understand.

People would *really* think I'm crazy if I shared the kind of things I think.

Life is like sitting in a movie theater watching horror movies. All of a sudden I become part of the picture. I can't get out; I can't even call out for help.

Sometimes when it gets to be too much I turn on the shower and cry so nobody can hear me. My wife would be devastated if she knew how hard I struggle each day just to keep on living.

I have lost myself and knowing that I have is the greatest blow of all. If I didn't know I think it would be easier to bear.

Think how stressful it would be if you could *never* let down your guard. If you had to keep "outward appearances" in force

24 hours a day. If, even with your closest friends and family members, you felt obliged to look, act, and feel as though everything were fine when on the inside you were wishing you could die. "Well," you say, "I thought that's what therapy was all about; so people with *those kind of problems* have a place to get rid of their unpleasant thoughts and feelings." Although psychotherapy provides a safe, nonjudgmental environment in which to share feelings and learn new coping skills, many never make it into therapy. They fear the stigma of being labeled "sick" or "mentally ill" so they continue to suffer in silence. Or they can't afford private psychiatric care and can't bear the thought of returning to an overcrowded, understaffed state facility. Or they don't even know psychotherapy is an option. Individuals who do come in, at least initially, continue to safeguard their most shocking thoughts and feelings because they are afraid that even a professional therapist would be shocked or disgusted. They even fear the reactions of other patients because "nobody else could ever possibly like and accept me if they really knew me for what I am."

These individuals look normal, talk normal, walk normal, and generally keep themselves together until the stress of wearing this perpetual mask reaches a level where it is impossible to keep up the front. When it finally comes crashing down the results are often disastrous: suicide, attempted suicide, running away, or decompensating (falling apart) so severely that their only protection is hospitalization on a locked, acute care unit like Ward 312. This increases rather than decreases stress and confusion for the patient and family members. If only they could come out from behind this facade, at least in their own homes, all this might be avoided. Until social attitudes change, these individuals will continue to project what they think others want to see rather than who they really are: Real people, with real issues, feelings, and needs. Few of us so-called "normal" folks can relate to the idea of how devastating and exhausting it is to keep up this masquerade 24 hours a day, 7 days a week. The following analogies are designed to give you a sense of how it must feel always to be "on." To know that you can never let anyone know what you really think and feel—even when it results in self-destruction.

THE BRIDE

My wedding was a traditional Catholic wedding with all the trappings. I looked beautiful! My hair was carefully styled into a mass of curls that accented my neckline. My makeup was perfect, my nails long and flawless. The dress was soft and flattering. The bows joining the bodice to the skirt were just the right size. I wore pearl earrings and a matching necklace that belonged to my mother and bought shoes with baby seed pearls to coordinate with my ensemble. Even my pantyhose were beautiful. They had a little feminine design up one leg made from baby pearls and a matching garter provided the finishing touch. Yes, I looked beautiful and everyone admired me as I walked regally down the aisle to marry my dream man.

Now, let me tell you a little about myself so you can understand how my wedding day really went! I am a simple person who, until I began my professional career at age 30, wore dresses only to weddings and funerals. I never wore makeup and even now wear only the minimum required to look "professional." I wear long straight hair, and since I'm athletic, short, unpainted nails. This was my second wedding. My first occurred when I was 16 and I assure you it was much less formal. I had never been to a prom or any other occasion to get "all dolled up" for, so this transformation to the blushing bride was quite traumatic.

It all began several weeks before the wedding when I decided to grow real nails. I carefully nurtured them, wore gloves, and used a nail strengthener. The day before the wedding two of them broke off down to the quick and were beyond repair! I set up an appointment at the beauty parlor to have my hair put up in curls and my traitorous nails overlaid with false ones.

After 3 hours in the beauty parlor I left—beautiful and *very* stiff (I felt awkward with my "tall" hair, afraid of messing it up). Since I always wear short nails my beautician had to strap on my seatbelt for me. I went to the church and a friend did my makeup, so that part went fine. As I started to get dressed, I realized I would *never* get my pantyhose on with those long nails—my maid of honor had to pull them up for me! Yes, I *looked* beautiful on the outside, but on the inside I was a wreck. I felt like my hair would topple over at any time. The nails were so awkward I felt like a cat with tape on my paws. I managed to get through the experience looking beautiful, and have lovely wedding pictures and some funny stories to tell, but boy was I relieved to get back into blue jeans and a T-shirt!

Try to imagine having to go through this *every day of your life!* Having to look and act perfect: every nail perfect, every hair in place, clothes just right, makeup applied with just the right touch. Think about going through your daily routine like this. Washing dishes, vacuuming, mowing the lawn, playing with your kids, cooking, going to work, taking the dog to the vet. Boy would *that* be stressful, because if you did all those chores it's almost certain that at some point you would break a nail, mess up your hair, smudge your clothes. That is what people with mental illnesses must endure every day. All the things we take for granted become conscious efforts of self-control for them. They have to monitor what they think, how they feel, the kind of look they put on their face, the way they move, how they talk to others.

THE GLAMOUR OF HOLLYWOOD

Have you ever been to one of the movie studios in Southern California? I have a sister who lives there but I have never gone. I've always been fascinated by the polished and realistic nature of motion pictures and I'm afraid that seeing how it is *really* done will forever change the way I feel when watching a movie. In real life, casting directors struggle to select the "perfect" actor for each part. Actors spend hundreds of hours memorizing lines and practicing their delivery. Stage hands scurry about setting up and changing scenes. Special effects people strive to create those "realistic" sights and sounds that give each scene credibility. Makeup artists work diligently to hide "human flaws" that are intensified by the bright lights of movie cameras. Then there are budget issues, advertising and marketing, directors, assistant directors, cameramen, sound specialists. The list goes on and on. When the actual "shoot" occurs, the air is tense with anticipation and everyone secretly hopes that every scene can be completed in just one take. Despite the glamour and glory of Hollywood, this sounds like a *very* stressful way to spend each day. The good news is that each of these people can go home at night and be who they really are. Once the director says "Cut! That's a take," or "Cut! That's a wrap," those involved can shed their "professional roles" and slip back into "ordinary people" roles.

Now, imagine this scenario again, only this time the director never says "Cut! That's a take," or "Cut! That's a wrap." You must always be "on," ready to perform. Always smiling, walking, talking, and moving just the right way. You must remember each step of your respective role in the production of this movie that will never be finished. No taking off your "professional" role, no going home to the family, no vacations, weekends, or breaks. You must carefully monitor looks, gestures, and comments at all times. Mental and emotional illnesses cast individuals in permanent roles from which there is no escape. These individuals are forced to keep their facade intact at all times. The fear of being labeled, judged, or abandoned prevents them from taking off their "picture of health" roles. We rarely see the exhaustion, frustration, confusion, anxiety, fear that never being allowed to be yourself creates.

What's Your "Outer Limit"?

Remember those timed physical fitness tests in junior high and high school? You went to gym class, suited up, and were put through a series of activities to test your physical endurance and agility. Sit-ups, chin-ups, running the 50-, 100-, and 600-yard dash, the broad jump, rings, jumping-jacks, squat-thrusts. All to determine how much you could accomplish in the shortest amount of time. Then you received a fitness rating: where you stood in relation to others in your age group across the nation. Thank goodness this minitorture session only came around once a year and lasted a mere 1 or 2 hours! Yes, we can pretty well fake our way through that. Knowing something is time limited can provide just the right amount of motivation to get the job done (only x more minutes to go, only x more events, and then I can put this behind me).

Now, let's remove the time limit and make this an experience that never ends. You go to gym class, suit up, and begin the fitness test. The person in charge informs you that the rules have changed. You must complete the *entire* series of events over and over again for the rest of your life! Sounds a bit like something out of *The Twilight Zone* or *Night Gallery*, doesn't it? This is what it feels like to be mentally ill. Life is not simply something you live, it is on ongoing struggle, a desperate attempt to grasp that elusive state of being called "normal." No matter how hard they try, just before reaching the finish line, something else always happens. Somebody "finds out" about their mental illness, resulting in loss of employment, friends, and credibility as competent human beings. Symptoms increase, making it impossible to keep their illness hidden from the view of those to whom they are closest. They are forced to think about how "different they are" on a daily basis when taking medication, participating in therapy, having problems containing symptoms, and when trying to aspire to "the American dream": family, home, and career. Think about how you might feel if you knew beyond the shadow of a doubt that there is no turning back, that you could never become the person you might have been but for your mental illness and the symptoms it creates. All the shattered dreams, broken promises, disappointments, limitations, rejections from those who just don't understand. Quite a burden on top of the already heavy load called "daily life," wouldn't you agree?

THE HOLOGRAM

Holograms are wonderful 3-dimensional illusions that look so real you can almost touch them. They create images so real that we almost jump out of our seats. Adding sounds, smells, and physical sensations through the use of special effects further convinces moviegoers that the experience is real. If you have ever been to an IMAX theater you know what I'm talking about. You feel like the roller-coaster you are sitting in is real. But try and touch it—you can't. Or what about the helicopter ride over the Grand Canyon. Can't you feel the breeze in your hair, hear the blades of the rotor as they slice through the air, smell the gasoline fumes from the engine? Again, try touching this helicopter and it simply isn't there. What about going over Niagara Falls in a barrel? You hear the rush of water, the deafening sound when it makes contact with the rocks below. You have the sensation of spinning, turning, rolling that is so real it may cause you to get queasy or throw up. You may even smell the damp wood of the barrel, the water, the nearby trees. Despite this ability to trick the mind into believing holograms are real, they are illusions that don't exist without the presence of special effects.

The nice thing about holograms is that you can terminate them at any time. If it's a pleasant experience you feel refreshed and alive, almost sorry you must return to "the real world." If it's a scary experience, you leave feeling relieved that it was just an illusion. People with mental illnesses project a hologram called "the picture of health." They must create an image so real that it's believable. This leads to avoidance. If someone gets too close, they might discover the picture of health is simply an illusion behind which lurks the stigma of mental illness. This image is not something they can ever turn off because then people would "know." It's an image they desperately struggle to maintain 24 hours a day, 7 days a week. Imagine if *your* life was like a hologram and never for a minute were you able to share your true feelings and thoughts. You must always strive to create an illusion you *think* others might accept.

THE BROKEN THERMOS

Do you remember the old timey thermos bottles that were metal on the outside and glass on the inside? They were great! When I was a child my parents took my sisters and I to the drive-in movies. This was an inexpensive way to coordinate family outings. To make it even more fun, my mother always took along sacks of popcorn and thermos bottles filled with hot chocolate for the kids and coffee for the adults. It was great unless with all the horsing around a thermos got broken. The bad thing about old timey thermoses is that if you drop them, the glass insides shatter into a million pieces. Yeah, the broken thermos still LOOKS okay because the metal casing is intact, but if you look inside it's a mess. You can never use the thermos again, even if you remove the broken glass, because then it has no mechanism for keeping things hot.

Living with a chronic mental illness is much the same. You still "look" okay on the outside because your body (casing) is intact, but if you look inside it's a mess! Jumbled thoughts, raw emotions, problems processing information, changes in chemistry. Imagine what it must feel like to look so normal that nobody believes you're really sick. To have people judge you, question you, poke, prod, and cajole you into trying things you know are no longer possible. Would you ask a quadriplegic to lift weights? Sounds kind of unrealistic, doesn't it? If their arms and legs don't work, how could they possibly lift weights? Well, what's so different about asking a person with paranoid schizophrenia to take a job working with people, or asking a person with posttraumatic stress disorder to accept a job in sales? They look okay, so what's the problem? Well, they look okay but just apply some stress and see what happens. This is a common occurrence for people with mental illnesses. Since most of them walk among us undetected, people find it hard to believe they are really ill. Think how you would feel if *you* were sick and nobody believed you.

THE SELF-CLEANING OVEN

All my life I wanted a self-cleaning oven. I was so tired of spraying, scrubbing, scraping, and fussing over conventional ovens when they got dirty. When my husband and I bought our new house I was very excited—it had a self-cleaning oven. Although the house was 20 years old, the realtor billed it as "a home with many upgrades and special features." It looked great and this oven was begging me to become its owner. I noticed the oven had a piece of foil under the heating coil and thought that odd since it was self-cleaning, but the house had been inspected by an electrician so I chalked up my uneasiness to "buyer's anxiety." After we had been in our new home about 3 months the oven had accumulated enough dirt that I thought it was time to try out its awesome self-cleaning feature. I pulled up the protective screen, set the timer for 3 hours, and went about my merry way. Three hours later I returned. I opened the oven and guess what—it was still dirty. I couldn't believe my eyes! I convinced myself that it must have been dirtier than I thought so I reset the timer for 5 hours and tried again, confident that this time it would do the job. Well, you can imagine my disappointment when I checked after 5 hours and it was still dirty! So much for a self-cleaning oven, I guess looks really can be deceiving.

Let's go a step further. Imagine buying a house that looks great and then falls apart piece by piece. You open a door and the knob falls off. You close a door and sheetrock on the adjacent wall crashes to the floor. You open the shower door and it breaks off at the hinges. Your oven doesn't heat, the connection for your gas logs is loose, the hot water heater goes out, and so on. But the house *looked* so solid! Mental illness is much the same. Outward appearances reflect strong, healthy looking people who seem intelligent and motivated. How can they look and sound so good if they are ready to fall apart at the slightest touch? Again, looks can be deceiving and often are. This frustrates those with mental illnesses as much as it does the people who criticize them. If I can think a thought, why does it get all confused when I try to express it to others? Why when I try to work do I have crushing anxiety attacks? Why when I know I have certain tasks that have to be accomplished do I lie cemented to my bed unable to get up? Why, why, why? The answer: symptoms of each mental illness disable the bearer in one way or another. Although they are intelligent and motivated people, the connection between thoughts and actions short-circuits before they can mobilize their plans. The simplest tasks become impossible, contributing to an ever growing sense of self-hatred and shame. How would you cope with looking so good on the outside all the while knowing if somebody "tests the equipment" it will fail dismally? Let's look at one final analogy before moving on.

THE ALIEN

I'm sure you've seen science fiction movies where invading aliens assume a human form so they can walk undetected among their unsuspecting victims. These aliens change shape and appearance at will, always staying one step ahead of their intended prey. In some cases, when they get wounded or go to sleep, they automatically revert to their "true form" which leaves them vulnerable to attack. Mental illness is much the same. Individuals with mental illnesses assume "the picture of health" so they can walk undetected among their fellows. They generally succeed in staying one step ahead of being "found out"; however, when they experience an increase in symptoms, or face stressful situations, they automatically revert back to their "real selves" which leaves them vulnerable to ridicule and rejection. How difficult to wear a mask that can remove itself suddenly, with no warning, leaving the wearer exposed to the scrutiny of others who may not understand. It's no wonder people with mental illnesses are so fearful of discovery!

"Well" you say, "what happens to people with mental illnesses when they can no longer manage to project the picture of health?" There are several possible outcomes: They get sicker, die, or retreat into self-imposed prisons called social isolation. Unable to cope with the inability to "be normal and fit in" they silently slip away, hiding their pain and frustration from the world's view. This "masquerade of the caveman" is the essence of chapter 4.

CHAPTER 4

THE CAVEMAN

Remember the old cartoon series *The Flintstones?* Fred, Wilma, Pebbles, Barney, Betty, and Bam-bam? These prehistoric folks lived in little stone houses in Bedrock. Fred and Barney worked at the rock quarry and Wilma and Betty were traditional housewives. They had television, bowling alleys, dinner clubs, and other amenities of the "modern" stone age world. Cars were foot powered. Large dinosaurs were used as cranes, buses, and other work related vehicles, and small dinosaurs became household pets. It's a cute series and reruns air almost every day, so watch it if you haven't had the pleasure.

This portrayal of prehistoric times, although funny, is about as far out as you can get. My hunch about real cavepeople is that life was much less comfortable. They lived in caves and survival was the main order of the day. No cars, no televisions, no Bedrock bowling alley, no local supermarkets. Danger lurked at every turn so outings were limited to those essential for survival: hunting, gathering, and mate selection. Life expectancy was very short even for those who didn't get eaten by predators. Accidents, disease, and hard living ended most lives well before 30. Thank goodness times have changed; I'm pushing 40 so I would be long gone!

Think how challenging it must have been to live in prehistoric times. Cut off from the larger world, unaware of all that

existed beyond "the survival zone." No vacations across coun-
try to visit the relatives, no trips to fancy resorts, no neighborhood hangouts. With survival as the primary goal, life must
have been very grim: It would have focused *entirely* on how to
get through just one more day alive. I don't know what these
people thought about, but I bet it was pretty basic. Personal
growth, education, and career advancement were not even possibilities. Life in the 20th century is so much easier—isn't it?

For most modern folks life involves much more than basic
survival. We aspire to the American dream, always trying to get
just a little closer to having it all: family, career, opportunities
for play and relaxation. What about those among us with mental illnesses? They dream the same dreams, but like their prehistoric predecessors remain focused on basic survival: how to get
through just one more day alive. Those who can no longer
project the picture of health retreat into their private hells,
grimly struggling for survival. There is no joy in living. Each
new day is a painful reminder of what they are missing, of how
different they are from "normal" people. Mr. J is an example
of just how grim life can become.

Mr. J came into treatment at age 55. He suffers from obsessive–compulsive disorder. Individuals with this mental illness
have thoughts that are automatically replayed until they participate in some behavior to make the thoughts go away. Typical
examples are checking and rechecking locks, counting money,
washing and rewashing their hands, counting steps as they walk,
and so on. This pattern of thinking and behaving severely limited Mr. J's life. He never married and chose a career that
allowed him to hide his behavior (he was a merchant marine
and spent most nights checking and rechecking the day's work
to make sure he had done it correctly). As he grew older, his
symptoms increased making it more and more difficult to hide
his behavior. He finally retired and moved into a small apartment in downtown Houston.

Most of Mr. J's day was spent washing, ironing, counting,
and sorting his money. One of his obsessive thoughts was that

he had to spend money in order, oldest money first, or something terrible would happen. This money had to be carefully washed, and if paper money, it had to be ironed. Can you imagine how it would feel to go to the store for a newspaper and *have to* spend 30 minutes standing in front of the vending machine organizing your change so you could *guarantee* you were spending the oldest coins first? Remember, in his mind, a mistake would result in deadly consequences. This simple task often took up most of his morning. Then there was lock checking, organizing things in perfect order, only being able to ride the bus if there was an odd number of people on it. This is the same gentleman I spoke of in chapter 3 who felt compelled to wipe fingerprints off *everything* guests touched to prevent their deaths from heart attacks.

Mr. J's entire existence was spent thinking obsessive thoughts and frantically trying to counteract them with compulsive behaviors. He had no time or energy for personal growth, relationships, family, home, or career. Each day was a desperate struggle for survival and time not spent on obsessive thoughts or compulsive acts was spent attempting to hide this behavior from others. He finally sought professional help when he reached a point where he could not even force himself to go out for groceries, he had them delivered. He realized that if his behavior continued, it would finally reach a point where he would not even be able to answer the door to accept his groceries.

Treatment was very difficult for Mr. J. He enrolled in the Day Hospital program and was scheduled to attend a variety of groups 5 days a week between 8:00 A.M. and 2:00 P.M. This required him to awaken at 3:00 A.M. so he could complete all his rituals before coming in for the day's activities. Riding the bus was a challenge since he always had to make sure the number of people on the bus added up to an odd number. Buying lunch was difficult because he had to organize his money so he spent old money first (all the while trying not to draw attention to himself). Things had to be organized *perfectly* or his anxiety would become so intense he thought he was dying.

Part of Mr. J's treatment involved medication to reduce his obsessive thoughts and compulsive behaviors. He also learned coping skills to get through stressful experiences without activating obsessive thoughts and compulsive acts. Some of his assignments involved riding the bus without counting people, spending money out of order, creating a mess and forcing himself not to clean it up, not wiping fingerprints off household items when he had guests. Group therapy was a powerful tool since other patients offered encouragement and support when he felt hopeless. Mr. J made progress in therapy, but will always have to monitor his thoughts and behaviors, struggling against urges to participate in senseless and unproductive rituals. He continues to be more isolated than is healthy, and will never have what most of us consider a "normal" life, but can at least accomplish the basic tasks of daily living. Think how difficult it must be for people like Mr. J.

Mr. J is not alone in his struggle for survival. Millions of mentally ill Americans spend their lives just trying to get through another day. My sister was one of them. She used huge amounts of energy trying to create an image she and others could accept and live with. When this became impossible, she retreated into self-imposed isolation to hide her symptoms. The shame and hopelessness that followed, even in the presence of a loving family, was not enough to prevent her death. Each year thousands of people just like my sister become casualties in a war called mental illness. Many of these victims are hidden from view making it easier for us to rationalize that it really isn't such a big problem after all. The following analogies are designed to help you understand just how serious this life-and-death struggle becomes for these "invisible" casualties.

SLEEPING BEARS

Bears have always amazed me. They eat huge amounts of food then sleep through the brutal months of winter. To conserve fuel their breathing and heart rates drop dramatically. They sleep peacefully, oblivious to the harsh elements outside their caves. When spring arrives they awake, thin but none the less healthy, new cubs at their side. Adult bears spend the next 8 or 9 months teaching survival skills to their young then, once again, retreat into hibernation. This cycle repeats itself year after year, providing not only tools for survival but a source of renewal and growth.

What if we apply the concept of hibernation to humans? What about long periods of self-imposed isolation to replenish the species? The first flaw is that humans do not have the capacity to sleep for extended periods of time without experiencing negative consequences. Even those in coma must receive intravenous nutrition and be repositioned regularly to protect tendons and muscles from atrophy. When I worked as an aide in a nursing home I witnessed the consequences of long-term inaction. Residents became depressed and emotionally withdrawn. Their bodies withered away to 70 or 80 pounds, muscles atrophied, tendons shrunk drawing arms and legs into fixed positions that rendered them useless. Their quality of life was extremely limited. Many were mentally alert, painfully aware that their bodies had become prisons from which the only escape was death.

Mental illness creates a similar scenario. Locked away in prisons of isolation, these individuals, unlike sleeping bears, are very much aware of their plight. They know life is going on just beyond their doors, but lack the ability to join in activities that typify daily life: jobs, family activities, personal pleasures. Like wild animals in cages, these desperate individuals pace back and forth unable to escape their symptoms. Unlike the hibernation of bears, this form of hibernation never ends. Spring never arrives, there is no new life, no rejoicing. Life becomes a perpetual state of winter: dark, grim, and lonely. Each day is as bleak and hopeless as the one before.

Suspended Animation

My best friends are "trekkie" fans. They never miss an episode of *Star Trek*, the show about space travelers. These space travelers journey through the galaxy on the starship *Enterprise*. During extended periods of travel crew members are placed in a state of suspended animation to "freeze time." Although hundreds of years may pass, they awaken essentially unchanged, unless of course their suspension capsule ruptures! When this occurs, survivors discover the dried up remains of their unfortunate colleagues.

Humans have always been fascinated by eternal life and we are forever seeking ways to extend life and revive the dead. The whole concept of cryogenics (freezing the dead until a cure for their illness can be discovered and administered and their life restored) speaks of our refusal to accept mortality as an inevitable part of the life cycle. At least in *Star Trek* time travelers are unconscious when suspended, unaware that time is passing. Even those who die, do so in sleep, unaware of what they have lost. Those frozen after death in the hope of being cured and revived in the future are equally unaware, so if revival doesn't happen they will never know.

What about the mentally ill who are suspended in isolation? Frozen by their symptoms, unable to move beyond the confines of their homes? Are they equally unaware? Do they slip into a state of being that protects them from the reality of their situation? The answer is *no!* They are *painfully* aware that life is passing them by. If unaware they would not experience the intense emotional pain that comes from knowing, full well, that they are not and most likely will never be a part of mainstream society. This reality prompts many to end their lives. Much like being paralyzed with curare, the victim is aware but unable to move. How horrifying to be aware yet unable to act.

THE MIRAGE

Have you ever seen a mirage? They are *very* convincing. In the desert, heat reflecting off vast expanses of sand creates illusions that appear quite real until you walk right up to them. People lost in the desert have been known to drink sand thinking it is water. The desperate desire to survive clouds their ability to distinguish illusion from reality. If someone tries to prevent them from drinking sand, they will fight to the death, steadfastly believing the sand is water. Thank goodness modern forms of travel have drastically reduced the incidence of this kind of tragedy.

"So," you say "what does this have to do with mental illness?" Many mental illnesses distort the reality of affected individuals. Perception merges with reality making it difficult to determine what is real and what is a byproduct of mental illness. This distorted thinking gives rise to a difficult dilemma: to venture beyond the familiar often produces an immobilizing level of anxiety. The fear of dying or meeting with some unspeakable horror creates an invisible force field from which they cannot escape. Even when others offer reassurance that the world beyond their home is "safe," they cannot make themselves believe it is true. The perception of danger, just like the belief that sand is really water, is so strong they will often choose self-neglect and death over social interaction. Even when not life threatening, these perceptions often result in social isolation, damaged self-esteem, and severely limit individuals' ability to effectively participate in social, family, and employment arenas. Trapped by the imaginings of their minds, these individuals face a double bind. "If I challenge my perceptions I must face and go through the terror they create with no guarantee things will be better on the other side. If I avoid this task, my life will become more and more restricted until the joy of living is squeezed out of me much like a boa constrictor squeezes the life out of a mouse."

For individuals experiencing perceptual distortions, change cannot occur until the pain of being socially isolated exceeds their fear of change. Even then intense fear drives many back into the uncomfortably familiar before they have an opportunity to determine whether different is better or worse. How frightening to be so unsure of yourself that you never know whether to believe what you think or feel, or even what you see. It is kind of like being blind and trying to decide whether the next step leads to safety or danger. If nobody else is around you have to decide whether to keep standing there or take a step and hope you make the right choice. I sure wouldn't want to be in those shoes—would you?

The Soundproof Room

One of my friends is a musician. He has a soundproof room in his home filled with musical equipment. He can spend hours in this room, playing his guitar or keyboard, without bothering other family members. It's a nice form of escape for him since his career as a psychiatrist is very stressful. He can get into his music and forget about the world outside. When you are in a soundproof room you can't hear what's going on outside nor can others hear what you are doing. You are insulated from the world, alone, surrounded only with the sounds of your own creation. Sounds like a nice break from reality, doesn't it?

Now apply this concept to someone who is mentally ill. The symptoms of their illness prevent them from sharing thoughts and feelings with others. They insulate themselves from the world to avoid hurting others and to reduce the risk of being ridiculed or shunned. Like the musician in the soundproof room, they are cut off from those around them. They can't reach out for the help they need and nobody can hear their silent screams. They are alone, surrounded by their distorted perceptions of reality. Unlike the musician who experiences a nice break from reality, these individuals feel trapped. Although screaming on the inside they can't be rescued since nobody on the outside can hear them. What a horrifying way to live.

Buried Alive

When I was a child I watched a movie in which a busload of school children were kidnapped and buried alive. Their captors planned to keep them until ransom demands were met. The children were buried longer than the kidnappers planned and began to run short on air. The movie was about their efforts to escape before dying from asphyxiation. I believe they did succeed in breaking free, but this movie made a lasting impression. For a long time I feared being buried alive. What if my parents *thought* I was dead and I was just in a coma. I would be unable to tell them and they would bury me alive! Then I would hear the dirt being shoveled onto my coffin, knowing that the air inside would soon be gone and I would suffocate and *really* die. Of course I never discussed my fears with my parents or even my siblings or friends. I thought they would laugh at me for thinking such foolish thoughts. When I got older I realized that since people are embalmed before being buried this terrifying experience was not even a remote possibility. I laugh when I think about how worried I was about coming to such a gruesome end.

Let's add a twist to this tale. Individuals whose mental illnesses create symptoms severe enough to force them into isolation are, in fact, buried alive. Locked away from the world's view, they silently wait for someone to realize they need help, and quickly, before they *really* die. Since they are hidden from view, nobody notices their frantic struggle for survival: Bottles of pills beg to be swallowed; loaded guns, like magnets, draw them closer and closer toward death. Razor blades, sharp and shiny, promise an end to the agony of life. Do you find this shocking? It is the reality of many Americans on a daily basis. The isolation they endure to hide symptoms contributes to the downward spiral that can only end in depression and/or death. They *know* their risk of dying increases with each passing day, and for some, life becomes the enemy and death a welcome friend. They slowly and painfully slip away from those who, if they only knew, might interrupt this deadly process. What a tragic end for so many who might be saved if only someone knew how desperately help was needed.

The Lost Child

My youngest son, now almost 4, is both vision and hearing impaired. Unlike "normal" 4-year-olds, he cannot tell you his name, where he lives, or who his parents are. His vocabulary is so limited he can't even tell me what happened when he gets hurt. Although we are learning sign language, it will be a long time before he can successfully communicate in a hearing world. This has been anxiety provoking for me since I work full time and he is in daycare. I took great pains selecting daycare where I felt he would be fairly treated. Things were going along just fine until he turned 3 and began deaf education classes. This requires him to ride a bus back and forth between school and his daycare. I had horrible visions of him being "misplaced" and never getting back to us since he doesn't know who he is. One day while discussing this issue with my daycare provider one of the other mothers, a police officer, offered to get an identification bracelet for my son. She said, "Fill out these forms, get me a lock of his hair and a picture, and we'll set up a file for him at the station. If he gets lost, the bracelet has the station's phone number and a 4-digit I.D. number that when entered in our computer lists everything from who his parents are to what specific disabilities he has." I quickly completed the paperwork and feel *much* better now Vincent has a lifeline that, in the event he should ever get lost, could bring him back to me.

Mental health care provides a similar lifeline for the mentally ill. There are medications to reduce symptoms, classes that teach people how to identify and cope with symptoms medication cannot remove, peer support groups for encouragement, and mental health professionals to provide a safe, nonjudgmental setting in which the damaging effects of mental illness can be counteracted. I would have been crazy to turn down the police officer's offer of an I.D. bracelet for my son, so why do so many individuals with mental illnesses fail to access an equally valuable lifeline? Many have symptoms so severe they simply cannot reach out for help so they are never identified. Some, fearing the stigma of being labeled, elect to suffer in silence. Others remember movies like *One Flew Over the Cuckoo's Nest* and are afraid of being turned into zombies. Many have had negative experiences with mental health professionals in the past and are afraid of a repeat performance. There are as many reasons as there are people, but the end result is the same: the risk of negative consequences unless their symptoms are stabilized and sources of support identified. Just as my son needs added measures to ensure that, if lost, his identity will be known, those with mental illnesses need a safety net to ensure they get safely through psychiatric crises. Imagine the panic my son would feel if he got lost and could not tell anyone his name or how to find those who love him. Imagine feeling your life is falling apart and nobody around you even notices; that you are calling out for help but no one can hear you.

I hope you are beginning to understand how difficult life is for those who can no longer project the picture of health and who, out of desperation, choose isolation to avoid rejection and ridicule. Since this group of patients is so quiet, we seldom give them a second thought. We make the same mistake that we make with cooperative children. How often do parents put down a phone to spank a naughty child? Now, how often do they put down the phone to praise an obedient child? I guarantee you we all pay much more attention to someone who is creating irritation in our lives and gratefully ignore those who are not! For isolated mentally ill patients this can mean the difference between life and death. Those who are loud and aggressive are identified and committed to locked wards, safe-guarded until their crisis resolves. Those who are silent go un-noticed, dramatically increasing their risk of suicide.

At this point we have identified two disguises frequently used to mask mental illness: the picture of health and social isolation. At one extreme are those who struggle to project an image that allows them to walk undetected among "normal people." At the other those who vanish, hoping to avoid creat-ing additional emotional pain for themselves and others. There are some for whom neither of these strategies works. They re-sort to equally desperate measures. Some use humor to distract themselves and others from looking too closely at their pain. Many wear a mask of anger to ward off concerned others who, if they got close enough, might expose the pain and confusion that lies just beneath the surface. Still others desperately cling to outgrown roles trying to recapture a time in life when they felt more in control. We will look at each of these disguises before book's end since all produce deadly consequences.

Although each disguise creates an illusion to distract from symptoms of mental illness, one of the most challenging, for me, is the use of humor. Individuals who rely on humor are forever laughing, joking, and changing the subject. This gener-ates frustration and anxiety for those attempting to intervene on their behalf. The complexity of this disguise merits close observation; therefore, chapter 5 introduces you to the people behind this mask: tortured souls who literally laugh themselves to death.

CHAPTER 5

TEARS OF A CLOWN

As a child one of my favorite treats was a visit to the circus. I was fascinated by the opening parade with its grand procession of costumed performers and gaily decorated horses, elephants, and dogs. I sat, mesmerized by the tightrope walkers, bareback riders, lion tamers, jugglers, and elephant acts. I loved the bright lights, exotic smells, and sounds that can only be found inside the magic walls of a circus tent. Yes, I loved everything about the circus, but best of all I loved the clowns: big clowns, little clowns, clowns in cars, clowns with dogs, juggling, jumping, doing cartwheels across the ring. They had red hair, purple hair, green hair, rainbow hair, big noses, and little noses. They wore funny hats, silly hats, tall hats, and short hats. Their costumes were always bright and colorful with enormous shoes that made them stumble and lurch when they walked. Their faces were the most intriguing: painted bright white, then outlined with an array of colors that created happy eyes, sad eyes, smiles, frowns, and other expressions designed to delight the audience. Yes, I loved clowns the best of all.

As a child I never wondered about the people inside those silly suits, faces painted to disguise their true identity. Like most kids, I thought clowns were always clowns, forever cast in roles with brightly painted faces and smiles that never wore off. By the time I reached adolescence I began to wonder what clowns were really like once the makeup came off and costumes were removed. I wondered if their lives were as exciting and glamorous as they looked. After all, they traveled to all sorts of exotic places and spent their time making others laugh. I wondered if they were always happy or if, like the rest of us, they sometimes felt the weight of the world on their shoulders. I never got close enough to ask a clown these questions, but as an adult, I now know that being a clown, like any other role, requires individuals to put on a mask congruent with their "public" identity. And like the rest of us, even clowns must deal with the realities of life, both good and bad, when their masks are removed.

Removing our masks to reveal *real* feelings is very difficult because from early childhood we are taught to present an image that pleases others or at least doesn't make them feel worse. In other words, if your thoughts and feelings might upset others, keep them to yourself! Happiness is part of the American dream. We created hundreds of catchy little phrases to remind ourselves not to share feelings unless we can make others laugh or feel better. When someone asks, "How are you today?" how many times do you respond, "Doing great, thanks!" even when you really feel awful? If you're like most of us, it's a standard response. Why do we play this game of looking and acting happy when we're not? Let's look at some of the phrases that prompt us to "put on a happy face."

> Fake it, 'til you make it.
> Smile: It will make people wonder what you've been up to!
> Laugh and the world laughs with you, weep and you weep alone.
> Keep a stiff upper lip.
> Sometimes you have to laugh to keep from crying.
> Don't worry, be happy.
> Everyone loves a clown.
> Laughter is contagious.

Although, at times, these phrases can be quite uplifting, we often get carried away, applying them indiscriminately to all situations. We forget that good mental health requires balance: We have to laugh some, cry some, work some, play some. When we get into a habit of using humor to camouflage emotional pain, we lose sight of the need to deal with the issues it is masking. Does this mean all humor is really a mask for emotional pain? Of course not! What I am saying is that when humor is used to escape the realities of life, it becomes a grim, joyless activity; an act of desperation designed to keep us one step ahead of our pain and fear. The cost: We lose the ability to experience *real* happiness and joy.

Although misdirected humor can create negative consequences for everyone, the results are devastating for those with mental illnesses. Think how overwhelming it would be to feel so depressed you can't imagine living even one more day—then your wife walks in so you smile and act "as if" everything is fine. Or you're sitting with a gun in your hand preparing to commit suicide when your child runs into the room, arms outstretched, shouting "Daddy! Daddy! I love you Daddy!" You quickly hide the gun, put on a smile, and pretend all is well. Or voices in your head torture you with vile and evil messages, yet when others are around you smile and pretend things are going great. This denial of pain is, in reality, an attempt to convince ourselves even more than others that we *are* happy and doing well. The consequence: If no one can see your pain, it grows, like a cancer, slowly eroding the slender thread that separates life and death. Projecting an image of happiness when in emotional agony moves victims deeper into isolation and despair, greatly increasing the risk of self-destructive behavior or death. Let's look at a real life example which, tragically, ended in suicide.

Mr. K was a patient with multiple psychiatric diagnoses. Reared in an abusive family, he was frequently beaten as a child and learned to use humor to mask his terror. As an adolescent he watched in horror as his brother drowned, knowing there was nothing he could do. During the Vietnam War he experienced the deaths of many friends and saw horrible acts of human destruction. Then he suffered a terrible accident in which his face and hands were burned, features melted into a grotesque mask that even the most skilled plastic surgeons could not repair. Mr. K used drugs and alcohol to ease his emotional pain and relied on humor to keep others from seeing how desperately wounded he really was. When asked how he was *really* doing he always responded, "I'm doing just great! How about you?" Even in group he laughed, joked, told stories, and generally disrupted sessions when issues got too close to his pain. Neither therapists nor fellow patients could break through this wall of humor that so thinly masked his distress. Several weeks before his death he came to group happy and full of puns and stories. He denied feeling depressed, even when group members pointedly told him they knew better—Mr. K went home that night and tried to burn himself to death. He ended up on a locked unit, steadfastly claiming, "It was just an accident" as he flashed his charming smile. Once stable he was released and returned to outpatient groups with his shield of humor on full alert. The last time we saw Mr. K he was smiling and laughing, denying the enormous pain he had accumulated during a lifetime of traumatic experiences. Mr. K overdosed on drugs that week. It was a tragic end to a person who, although in tremendous pain, could not come out from behind his mask to seek the help he so desperately needed. I tell you his story to make you think. Mr. K is not alone. Many individuals with mental illnesses play this desperate game, and many, like Mr. K, end up dead. Let's look at some analogies to help you get a better feel for what can happen when humor isn't funny anymore.

THE MASCOT

If you know anything about chemical dependence you have probably heard the term *survival roles*. This term refers to roles family members unconsciously play to cope with the addict or alcoholic's behavior. The mascot is one of these survival roles.

This person is forever cracking jokes, laughing, jumping up and down, and generally acting like a clown. Although outsiders might describe the mascot's behavior as funny or immature, the person cast in this role feels trapped in a nightmare from which they cannot awake. In this nightmare people are laughing, and for a few minutes, it makes everyone "forget" about the family's desperate struggle against the monster called addiction. As the spell cast by the mascot's antics wears off, family members return to their desperate struggle. The mascot, feeling compelled to distract the family from its distress, immediately introduces his or her next humorous act. Like a hamster on a wheel, the mascot must continue to laugh, joke, and act silly because if this charade ever stops, the family secret will be exposed. The terror that comes with *knowing* you must keep on laughing no matter what to keep "*the truth*" from destroying your family must be stifling!

Individuals with mental illnesses feel much like the mascot in an addicted family system. Because symptoms of their illnesses often create family crises, they feel compelled to distract the family with humor. Once engaged, this never ending cycle of laughter becomes a deadly game that prevents them from sharing real feelings, sometimes to the point of self-destruction. Although they desperately want to stop laughing, they are afraid of damaging those they love so they continue this frantic masquerade. Think how it would feel *believing* that you have to keep laughing to prevent your family's destruction. The sense of panic when you reached a point where you simply could not keep on laughing, no matter what the consequence.

TICKLE TORTURE

Sometimes it's fun to roll around on the floor with someone you love and have tickle fights. I have three sons and when they were small the whole family got involved. Everyone got a turn at tickling and being tickled. This was a fun game because the tickling stopped as soon as someone said they'd had enough. Being tickled can be fun, but if it goes too far, it can become painful and frightening. At first, it is funny and makes you laugh—then it becomes uncomfortable. If it continues, it starts feeling painful. Beyond pain it can result in vomiting and involuntary release of urine or feces. Further still, it becomes a true form of torture.

Forced humor creates much the same consequence for those with mental illnesses. In the beginning it feels good to "put on a happy face." It makes your family feel good, and for awhile, you might even believe everything is going to be okay. As time passes, it becomes uncomfortable to hold up your "happy mask" when inside you are really miserable. If it continues, it creates emotional pain that must be worn inside out, hidden from view. Beyond pain it increases symptoms of one's illness. Further still, it leads to self-destructive acts and/or suicide attempts. This form of humor doesn't sound very funny, does it?

Sitcom Mania

Have you ever listened to the background laughter they play in most television sitcoms? Every time Lucy does something a bit bizarre in an episode of *I Love Lucy* canned laughter is activated to trigger an audience response. Or how about *Bewitched?* Samantha twitches her nose and something funny happens. Again, canned laughter appears prompting the audience to generating some real laughter. One of the newer shows, *Seinfeld,* plays interesting sounds along with the canned laughter for an even greater effect. Next time you watch a sitcom, listen to this laughter. The closer you listen, the more unnatural it sounds. It appears on cue, immediately following a funny event, and ends just as abruptly after 20 to 30 seconds. If you really listen, it has an artificial quality. Nobody laughs on cue in the "real" world.

Genuine laughter often starts unexpectedly, bursting forth without warning. Many times it stops, starts, stops, and starts again as the person laughing goes from laughter to giggling, and then laughs at how funny their laughter is. This happened to me when I watched the movie *Mrs. Doubtfire*. Robin Williams, dressed in his female disguise, accidentally caught his breasts on fire. He frantically slapped at these artificial breasts with a pot until the flames were extinguished. I started laughing, then tears ran down my face, then I laughed at how I could not stop laughing. I would stop laughing and suddenly start again when I thought about how silly this whole scene was. My laughter was spontaneous, not at all like the canned laughter that starts and stops with such predictability that it's like turning a faucet on and off.

When mentally ill individuals use humor to mask emotional pain, it has the same quality as the canned laughter in sitcoms. You don't notice the artificial quality of this laughter unless you really listen for it. These individuals are experts of disguise and are so convincing that, at times, they even fool themselves. The laughter that stems from desperation, when examined more closely, is frantic, almost hysterical in nature. The smile just a bit too bright, lasting a few seconds longer than it should. The laughter, forced, begins precisely when the individual most needs to distract those getting a little too close to his or her true feelings. This laughter occurs very suddenly, just like real laughter, but if you look closer, you see how controlled and intense it really is. After all, if your greatest fear is that someone might just see you for who you really are, it becomes very important to "put on a happy face." To generate this mask, the person must carefully construct an image of happiness and this is where, if you look closely, you can detect the subtle differences identified above. Think how difficult it would be to laugh and smile when, on the inside you are in a panic, wondering how soon you will lose the ability to keep up this front. The day will come when no matter how hard you try, others will see the desperation so carefully hidden behind your smile.

Halloween Goblins

My family really enjoys decorating for the holidays and Halloween is no exception. Each year I add a few new decorations, another stuffed goblin, a scary pot to put the candy in. Several years ago I saw two stuffed goblins that struck my fancy. One was a witch and the other a scarecrow. They were each about 18 inches high and made out of brightly colored, stuffed parachute material. Most intriguing of all was when you squeeze them, they emit a maniacal laughter that is both funny and scary. My youngest son likes to press the activating switch over and over again to hear this laughter. It really is funny, but what if the activating switch never shut off? What is these little stuffed goblins continued laughing 24 hours a day, 7 days a week. After awhile it wouldn't be funny anymore. It would become annoying, then irritating, then anger provoking, then maddening. Think about listening to this sound forever, with no way to turn it off or screen it out. "Oh" you say, "Just throw the damned things out, that will solve the problem." Well what if you couldn't throw them out, or if they magically reappeared, still laughing every time you thought they were gone for good. Think about how frustrating this would become, and how frightening. Being subjected to something that was slowly driving you crazy and having no way to control or stop it.

Many people who use humor as a shield against reality feel "as if" their off button has disappeared. Once the humor button is activated, it cannot be turned off. After all, if you work so hard showing others how well you are doing, how happy you are, how can you possibly go back and say, "Oh by the way, that was all an act, I'm really the most miserable person you ever met." This is too humiliating, too self-defeating, *so*, you just keep smiling, laughing, joking, teasing, screaming on the inside all the while. Like Mr. K, many struggle to keep up a front which they created without realizing that once in place, it could not be removed *unless* the wearer were willing to reveal his or her *real* feelings and thoughts. Most resist becoming real

due to the stigma attached to showing weakness in a society
that values independence and strength above all else. Think
how frightening it would be to know you have created an image
that must be maintained at all costs, even when it draws you
toward your own death.

THE STAND-UP COMIC

Stand-up comics are an interesting breed. They can be found
in comedy clubs, dinner theaters, lounges, and bars. Those who
make names for themselves appear on television and home
videos. The goal of a stand-up comic is simple: Make the audience laugh using whatever means possible. They tell stories,
crack jokes, and take jabs at famous people and political leaders. They often target controversial issues, carefully directing
comments to make us laugh at the things society elects to take
issue with. The beauty of watching a stand-up comic is, for a
little while, you can forget about reality and simply enjoy the
moment. These individuals remind us not to take life too seriously lest we lose sight of what is really important: love, laughter, and friendship.

Stand-up comics work hard. They must constantly revise material to keep it current and fresh. Audiences must be re-
searched to identify the approach best suited for a given group
of people so the end result is laughter not outrage. They must
carefully select their props and costumes, decide whether to
include a side-kick or fly solo. Since timing and presentation
is the essence of good comedy, they must diligently practice
their delivery, monitoring looks, voice tone and pitch, and body
language. A new routine requires hours of practice to increase
the chances of a smooth delivery. Yes, being a stand-up comic
is very hard work. When done well, the rewards of audience
laughter and approval are worth as much as the paycheck.
When done poorly, at least they have a paycheck and ideas
about what *not* to do next time. Best of all, being a stand-up

comic is a role, like any other job, that can be shed and left behind at the end of each day. Good or bad, at day's end, they can go home and be themselves. What if once their act started, it could never end; if their performance became a never ending litany of jokes, quips, and snappy remarks? Like my laughing goblins, at first it would be funny, then irritating, then anger provoking, and finally maddening for both the performer and the audience. Thank goodness this doesn't happen in real life—or does it?

People with mental illnesses often use humor as a defense against emotional pain. Like the stand-up comic, they strive to get their material "just right" to ensure the "right response" from family members and friends. Their goal: to produce an image of happiness so convincing that nobody would suspect what lies just beneath the surface. Wearing such a mask requires hours of practice to reduce the risk of being "found out." Like the stand-up comic, they must constantly practice their delivery, monitoring looks, voice tone and pitch, and body language. When done well, the rewards of family harmony and stability are worth the effort. When done poorly, consequences can be quite traumatic for all: suicide attempts, aggressive behavior, social isolation, family crisis, emotional instability.

Unfortunately, unlike the comic who can shed his or her role at the end of each day, individuals who wear this mask feel obligated to "keep up appearances" at all times. This becomes increasingly more difficult as time passes. Eventually, the pain behind the mask comes crashing through. Unlike the comic who can revise an act and try again another time, for these individuals, there *is* no opportunity for revision since the image has been shattered beyond repair. Exposed and vulnerable, they face the challenge of life without their mask, *if* they survive the experience.

If I have done my job well, you will never again see humor from quite the angle you did before reading this chapter. I don't mean to discourage you from laughing, or to imply that all humor is really a symptom of underlying emotional pain.

Humor is good and healthy when applied appropriately. It makes life more fun and less stressful. Only when humor is abused does it become dangerous and undesirable. Humor, like anything else, must be balanced. Good mental health means we have to give ourselves permission to laugh some, cry some, feel angry, joyous, afraid, sad, confused, hopeful, courageous, and a whole list of other feelings. If we begin to shut down feelings that are uncomfortable, we inevitably shut down those that are pleasant and soothing as well. Over time, we become shells filled with pain and confusion.

If you have learned nothing else from this chapter, I hope you have learned the importance of being true to your feelings. Laugh when things are funny and cry when they are sad. When you suspect someone you love is using humor to avoid dealing with other, more painful emotions, provide a safe and accepting environment so they may feel encouraged to take off their mask. In the next chapter we will look at a very different and, at times, a very frightening disguise: the mask of anger.

CHAPTER 6

THE PORCUPINE

When visiting the zoo I always feel sorry for the porcupines. They pace aimlessly back and forth in enclosures designed for maximum viewing pleasure with the least amount of risk to their human visitors. These visitors, fascinated by porcupines' impressive array of quills, often tease them to provoke a reaction. When a porcupine extends its quills in response to this human heckling everybody backs up, sure this "dangerous animal" is preparing for attack. Yes, porcupines have quills that can inflict a great deal of pain to the unlucky creature on the receiving end, but, have you ever taken a close look at a porcupine, I mean *really* looked at one? They're really not all that fierce looking if you look carefully past the quills. Porcupines are basically docile animals that release quills only when frightened or injured. I'm sure, if given a chance, porcupines would enjoy being petted and fussed over just like the rest of us. Since they are labeled "dangerous and unpredictable" nobody gets close enough to see the gentler side of these creatures.

Mentally ill individuals face a similar dilemma. Most are nonviolent, and even those who have angry outbursts are spurred on by emotional pain, fear, or confusion, *not* anger. They, like porcupines, are defined as "dangerous and unpredictable." Since John Q. Public only "sees" mental illness through the tinted glasses of social stigma they rarely get close enough to someone with a mental illness to see what they are really like. Comparable to the porcupine's threatening display of quills, these individuals activate defenses to reduce the risk of further rejection. They yell, gesture, threaten, and do all manner of things to keep those they *most* want to embrace at arms' length. These outward displays of anger are, in actuality, a defense against the fear, confusion, and emotional pain that lie just below the surface. And what of the individuals who turn their anger inward? Like an inside-out porcupine, the quills become a source of self-destruction that gradually destroys the individual from within.

"So," you ask, "how does one get close enough to befriend a porcupine, or an acting out mentally ill person, without getting injured?" My response: with patience, kindness, and caution! Willingness to see behind the mask we call anger is the first step. The second involves identifying and dealing with our own fear and uncertainty regarding the other person's hostile behavior. This helps us avoid the temptation to respond defensively. Since responding defensively only heightens the fear and confusion of a frightened or emotionally wounded person, the goal is to provide a safety net of acceptance and emotional stability until they are able to regain self-control and more appropriately express their feelings and needs. A case study will help illustrate this point.

THE ANGRY MAN

Mr. L suffers from posttraumatic stress disorder (PTSD) and major depression. He was in the clinic one day and became frustrated when he could not get a letter from his doctor the same day he requested it. He became very hostile and agitated so I took him into my office to see if I could calm him down. Once inside, he became even angrier, making negative statements about the government, his treatment team, and the Veterans Affairs Hospital in general. He suddenly lost control, screaming, yelling, jumping up and down, and in desperation, threw my phone. It crashed into the wall leaving a deep gash. By this time other staff members had become alarmed and "came to my rescue." They indicated the police would be called to contain the patient which only served to inflame him further. Since I know this patient well, I told him if he would pick up my phone and sit down, the police would not be called. He agreed and, with great difficulty, put my phone back on my desk and sat down. He was given some time to collect himself, then we explored where this rageful behavior was *really* coming from. I knew it was bigger than the identified "letter I can't get today." He began to talk about how helpless he felt, how once again his claim for disability benefits had been denied. He was tired of fighting the system, feeling inadequate as a provider for his family, and the *last straw* was not being able to get the letter he needed *immediately* (he saw this as yet another rejection). Mr. L began to cry and the deep sense of hopelessness masked by his angry outburst began to seep through. We spent another 45 minutes making plans for how he could identify his need for support in the future without becoming violent. He left, exhausted and relieved that I had not reacted to his defensive behavior by becoming defensive myself.

I can hear you thinking, "Well, Jo, you're a therapist. You're *supposed* to handle this kind of outburst without getting defensive." Let me tell you, I was *very* frightened during this episode! What helped me avoid a defensive response is my training in anger management and my knowledge of this patient's behavior across time (I knew he could become verbally abusive but had never actually hit anyone). By monitoring my *own* defensive reactions I was able to provide a safety net for his anger until he could identify his *real* feelings: fear, confusion, hopelessness, and despair.

Even as a trained therapist it was hard for me to avoid playing into his anger. Most people in similar situations become defensive. This makes it very difficult for the individual who is out of control to be supported through their crisis. "Porcupine behavior" keeps them from getting what they so desperately need: someone to see the person behind this mask, a person in such emotional pain they are reduced to instinctive defensive reactions. Keep this in mind the next time someone you love becomes hostile—what are they *really* trying to tell you? If you back up, be patient, offer support, and listen without judging, you may be very surprised at what you see beneath their mask of anger. The same is true for those who turn their quills inward as the next example will demonstrate.

THE QUIET MAN

Mr. M also has a diagnosis of PTSD and major depression. He, unlike Mr. L, turns his quills inward when feeling threatened or confused. He recently withdrew from family and friends, stopped eating, stopped attending therapy, and stopped taking his medication. As his symptoms worsened he became quieter and quieter. When asked to describe his feelings, he responded, "Everything is as it is so I plan to starve myself to death and set my family free." A closer look at his situation revealed intense anger at himself for failing to live up to the image of an adult male: employed, financially independent, a family provider. This became even more significant when cultural factors were considered: Mr. M is an American Indian and these values are the essence of his being. His inability to live up to these values made him feel like a burden to his family, and he came to feel that the only "honorable" thing to do was to starve himself to death and free them from the dead weight of his disabilities. Once this information was out in the open, Mr. M agreed to seek help. He had lost 50 pounds so he spent several weeks on a medical unit getting his health issues resolved. Once medically stable, he resumed his psychiatric medications and involvement in therapy. Although outward appearances were dramatically different from those of colorful Mr. L, the results were just as deadly. Mr. M was at great risk of death from self-neglect. The self-directed anger masked the *real* issue: his intense sense of failure as an Indian man.

As demonstrated above, misdirected anger can create life-threatening situations for mentally ill individuals and the people who love them. Failure to identify and remove this disguise allows the illness to progress and prevents others from getting close enough to help. As a clinical social worker my role is to help people identify, understand, and remove this disguise. In order to do this I have to teach individuals a more "acceptable" repertoire of response choices. When successful, the rewards are great: The person behind the mask is set free. Their true identity rises to the surface allowing them to become someone they, and others, love and respect. When unsuccessful, the costs are equally great: a downward spiral that further isolates the individual from desperately needed sources of support. I hope if you are masking a mental illness with anger you will seek help to uncover your true self. If you are a family member or friend, I hope you will seek help to better understand your loved one's struggle. If you are a mental health professional, strive to prevent defensive reactions from getting in the way when your clients most need your support and guidance. Let's look at some analogies to further illustrate the double-edged sword created by the mask of anger. The wearer's desperate desire for approval and understanding generates such fear they repeatedly strike out or withdraw once support is within arm's reach. Pay close attention, you may see yourself or someone you love!

THE PRICKLY PEAR

I had an encounter with a prickly pear when I was about 7 years old. I was playing chase in my front yard with friends and fell, hands first, into a family of prickly pear cactus. When I looked at my hands, they were covered with sharp needlelike quills. I ran to my mother in tears and she painstakingly plucked out the quills one at a time until they were all removed. I promise you I never played close to that cactus again! The cactus I fell into was not "angry" with me. It was protecting itself from further harm. Cactus plants, like people, have defense mechanisms to protect them from harm. Indeed, if we went around falling into cactus families and they had no way to protect themselves, they would eventually die. The cactus is endowed with sharp, spiny quills to deter potential sources of harm. Cacti, lucky for us, do not "think" about defending themselves. Their quills are automatically released when something, or as in my case, someone, runs into them. This defense is designed to preserve the species.

Humans, on the other hand, "think" about the events in their lives and form perceptions (ideas) about what these events really mean. This allows us to choose response choices to match the event (i.e., if you cut in line and I think it was an accident, I might say, "Excuse me, I was next in line." If, on the other hand, I believe you deliberately cut the line, my response might go more like this: "I beg your pardon! I was next in line and you need to step back and wait your turn like everyone else."). Unfortunately, many people "misperceive" the intention of events around them, overreacting in ways that anger, confuse, or frighten others. Individuals with mental illnesses are especially vulnerable to misperceptions because of past negative experiences and/or symptoms of their illnesses. Let's explore this further.

Individuals who react impulsively, without exploring options, generally select response choices that upset others. Most people get upset when someone begins yelling, gesturing, pacing, threatening, or throwing things. They also get upset when someone gets too quiet, broods, withdraws, or refuses to discuss the issue at hand. The *intention* of the person displaying anger reactions is to alert others that their needs are unmet. Unfortunately, what usually happens is that others *perceive* this defensive behavior as threatening or condescending. It's only a matter of time before the arm wrestling match begins: Who can become the nastiest or withdraw the furthest. Each time this type of exchange occurs it makes it more difficult for the person in need to make requests and for those who might be of help to extend a helping hand. This can lead to life-threatening consequences for someone experiencing suicidal or homicidal urges who does not know how to ask for help productively. Imagine desperately needing help and each time you tried to get someone's attention, you became mute, or they turned away and were unable to hear your cry for help. The harder you tried to obtain help the less available it became. Raging on the outside, screaming on the inside, unable to communicate the extreme nature of your need.

THE LADDER

Imagine that you are in an office on the 13th floor of a 20-story building. The building is on fire two floors below you and rapidly moving upward. Unable to escape by stairs or elevator, you climb to the top of the building and open the fire escape. You realize you are trapped and frantically look for a means of escape. Suddenly, you see a helicopter. The pilot activates his microphone and reassures you help is on the way, that you should stay where you are so the firefighters can rescue you. A wave of relief rushes over you *until* you hear a loud crash. The wall behind you has collapsed and the floor beneath your feet is beginning to buckle and get hot. Firefighters are forced to evacuate without you. The helicopter pilot once again offers encouragement and indicates he will try an air rescue. He drops a ladder from the side of the helicopter and instructs you to grab it, secure yourself as best you can, and hold on tight until safely on the ground. You are frightened but again, rescue becomes a possibility. You stand in the center of the roof, desperately trying to catch the ladder. The wind is strong and each time you think you have it, it is blown out of reach. Time after time you try and fail. Your mood becomes more frantic, then a grim determination to survive takes over. At last you succeed in grabbing the ladder and are whisked to safety, trembling with fear but alive.

Let's add a twist. Imagine you are trapped on top of this burning building and the helicopter pilot says, "I'll try an air rescue but with the winds, I may have to leave." You become frantic, desperate to survive. The ladder is let down and just as you are about to grab it, he pulls it up and flies away. You stand there in shock. The reality of your impending death sinks in. You don't stop to think that maybe the helicopter pilot is merely circling to get a better approach. You assume the worst: You have been abandoned. If he returns you will do *whatever it takes* to make sure he doesn't leave again without you. The helicopter returns and the pilot tells you he will try again, but you must follow instructions *exactly* to prevent him from crashing. You agree, secretly planning to grab the ladder regardless of what the pilot instructs you to do. He drops the ladder and you miss. He tries again and you get it, but he says, "You have to let go, the wind is picking up and I'll crash unless I back up *now*. I will make every effort to come back for you." Your fear generates anger and you steadfastly hold onto the ladder despite his pleas. Suddenly, a wind shear smashes the helicopter into the building. It bounces off, destroyed, and falls 20 stories to the ground below. It explodes on impact, killing both you and the pilot. If only you had listened! If only you could have moved beyond your fear and followed his instructions. *If only* never comes, you are dead!

This is much like the scenario that unfolds when an individual experiences a suicidal crisis. Trapped in what appears to be a never ending cycle of fear, pain, and confusion, the person blindly rejects the help of those trying to intervene. As efforts to save them intensify, their resistance increases. They lose sight of options, believing that suicide is the only way to end the pain. Life lines are thrown and repeatedly refused. Unable to move beyond their self-directed anger (quills turned inward) they see others' efforts as attempts to control rather than gestures of support. As this drama continues, they move ever closer to an inevitable suicide attempt. Those who are lucky survive. But many, like the desperate person on top of the burning building, simply cannot participate in their own rescue. They damage themselves or die, creating a legacy of pain for their survivors. Imagine how difficult it would be to so desperately need support yet be unable to reach out even when it is offered. How frightening to rush headlong toward death and be unable to interrupt your fatal course.

THE BULL

I have never understood how people can enjoy a bullfight. The poor bull is tortured by picadors until it is so weak and confused that the matador can practically walk right up to him for the kill. As a child I used to watch bullfights on television and get furious. My mother would ask, "Why do you watch that since it upsets you so?" I would reply, "Because I want to see a bull win." What I did not realize is that even if the bull "wins" (i.e., kills the matador) he is put to death and the meat donated to charity. People defend this gruesome sport by saying, "It's a fair contest: a 2,000-pound angry bull against a man with a sword." If we look closer, we see how it *really* is. A 2,000 pound bull who feels threatened and confused (and rightly so!) acting in self-defense. As he is chased, stabbed, and taunted, he becomes more and more frantic and confused. He snorts, paws, runs, attempts to gore, and stomps with murderous intent. Is the bull *really* mad? *No*, he is afraid for his life! How would you feel if someone chased you around, stabbing you? Like the bull, you would become defensive in a desperate struggle to survive. The bull, like the porcupine, the frantic man on top of the burning building, and the prickly pear cactus, is simply trying to survive. His aggressive actions are viewed as hostile and threatening, which "justifies" the matador's final act: killing the bull. He is killed for doing exactly what he *should* do in a life-threatening situation—fight for his life! Imagine if this happened to you.

Individuals who use hostile actions to defend against symptoms of mental illness are as compromised as the bull in a bullfight. Their actions, misunderstood, lead others to shun and ridicule them, increasing their sense of abandonment. The harder they try to make others understand, the more they are rejected or ignored. Hostile behavior is seen as "bad conduct" rather than a warning sign that they are out of control and desperately need assistance. Imagine how you might feel if you were frantically spinning out of control. You look around for someone, *anyone*, who might be able to help. Your efforts are misinterpreted as hostile acts causing others to back away. You yell, scream, and jump up and down, sure that if you make a big enough commotion they will understand the drastic nature of your situation. Instead, they look at you with hatred and fear. Confused, you become even more aggressive, *demanding* help. This simply creates greater resistance in others who will, quite literally, stand there and watch you disintegrate emotionally or turn and walk away. Imagine not knowing any other way to alert others of your pain. You were asking for help in the only way you know how and nobody understands.

THE OCTOPUS

Have you ever been to a marine park? They have seals, killer whales, walruses, and other sea animals that perform acts to delight and surprise visitors. Most marine parks also have huge aquariums with creatures from all over the world. I am always astonished by the octopi on display. These interesting creatures have no spines yet they travel through the water with amazing speed and agility. They are clever hunters who change color and form to blend in with their surroundings. Since their bodies are so fragile, their primary method of protection involves shooting "ink" then fleeing as this smoke screen shields them from their predator's view. The octopus is not angry when it ejects ink. It is afraid! People often say, "That octopus was so angry he's changed colors." Changing colors, like shooting ink, is merely a sign the octopus is feeling threatened. Octopi are not aggressive unless molested. They float along, minding their own business, eating what is necessary to survive, and not hassling others. They are quiet creatures, so they often go unnoticed unless they are stressed into a display of color change or ink ejection. People sometimes describe octopi as ugly or stupid because they fail to appreciate the unique qualities of this animal. People sometimes describe individuals with mental illnesses the same way, with devastating consequences.

Individuals who turn their anger inward, especially those with identified mental illnesses, tend to be ignored. People are so busy they focus on what calls loudest for their attention; the rest goes by the way. Unfortunately, this contributes to the corrosive nature of self-directed anger. Individuals who internalize anger go through life doing what is necessary to survive, locking away their fears, feelings, and needs. As their sense of futility grows, they come to believe they *are* stupid and worthless, that they are taking up space someone else could be using. They gradually withdraw from people and activities and others fail to identify the *real* reason for this self-imposed isolation: They are conserving energy for their struggle to survive. Unlike their aggressive counterparts, these individuals disappear from view, forgotten until some crisis creates self-destructive behaviors that others cannot help but notice. Let's look at an example of this process in action.

THE DESPERATE STRUGGLE

N was a woman who struggled constantly with thoughts of suicide. Major depression cast a shadow over her life, interfering with her ability to fully participate in family, career, and social arenas. N was a gentle and quiet person who blamed herself for life circumstances even when they were clearly beyond her control. She went through each day in silent desperation, hating herself for being ''less than functional'' in the eyes of society. After several failed suicide attempts, N quietly retreated,

chastising herself for not even being able to kill herself successfully. As time passed, thoughts of suicide and death became a
source of comfort, life a painful reality. She would rock along
for a few days or weeks then impulsively shoplift, use drugs, or
attempt suicide. This got a lot of attention from family members and friends, but each suicide attempt created a deeper
and deeper rift between N and the people who loved her. The
"ink" N relied on to hide her pain was impulsive behavior. She
participated in self-defeating behavior to get others' attentions,
but was unable to tell them *why* she needed their attention or
what they could do to help. Sadly, N did not escape her predator like the resourceful little octopus. Her predator lived within
and claimed her life tragically and unmercifully in her prime.
Yes, anger turned inward is dangerous; if you keep it inside it
can kill you, just as it killed N.

THE STEEL TRAP

Have you ever seen a hunter's trap? They are big, nasty looking
steel devices designed to hold their prey until the hunter returns to claim his prize. These traps have serrated teeth that
dig deep into the tissue of the trapped animal. Each time they
attempt to escape, the teeth dig a little deeper. This is an excru-
ciating process that can go on for days before causing death.
Animals have been known to chew off their own legs in order
to stop the pain. They will also indiscriminately attack anything
or anyone that approaches, regardless of the motive, because
they anticipate further pain. Trapped and helpless, they react
defensively out of pain and fear. These animals are not
angry—*they are afraid and in pain!* Any animal, including human beings, will react defensively under such circumstances.
Unfortunately, since others rarely understand the basis for their
behavior, they are treated with contempt. The more they struggle, the deeper becomes others' perception that they are just

"bad actors." This allows the pain to continue growing. Sometimes, in desperation, these individuals damage or kill themselves, just like animals caught in a steel trap. It is such a sad and dramatic ending when it could all be prevented *if only* they could identify their feelings and needs instead of withdrawing into self-contempt. Let's look at one final example before moving on.

THOSE EYES

Mr. O was diagnosed with paranoid schizophrenia. He had difficulty distinguishing fantasy from reality, was easily overwhelmed by sights and sounds in his environment, and heard voices on a daily basis that told him to kill or maim himself. He felt others were out to get him so he did not tell family members, or his doctor, when his symptoms were getting worse. This man was intelligent, therefore, *aware* of the devastating effects his illness had for himself and those he loved. He often blamed himself for being sick and felt God would punish him when the time was right. He retreated into his private hell, keeping his fear and pain guarded behind a wall of silence. The few times someone got close to his true feelings, he reacted with hostility before withdrawing behind his wall of silence. Mr. O was hospitalized many times for trying to kill himself. He burned himself, tried to jump from moving cars, and overdosed on medication. His final act of self-destruction was to remove both eyes and destroy them. Once blind, he felt he had paid penance for being sick and could now lead a "normal" life. Although a very sick person, Mr. O is not alone in resorting to drastic measures when the pain and fear of symptoms create self-directed anger seeking a path for escape. Like electricity, this anger "runs" until finally released. How sad it is that this man will be forever blind because his illness prevented him from asking for the help he so desperately needed.

I have painted a grim picture of the side effects created by the mask of anger. Please realize that not all anger is a mask for fear and emotional pain. As with humor, sometimes anger is justified and needs to be identified and expressed.The quality and nature of anger determines if it is genuine or a mask. If one's reactions appear too extreme given the circumstances (as with Mr. L), go on for too long, or seem "forced" or artificial, it is a warning sign that deeper issues lie just beneath the surface. The greatest gift we can give to ourselves and others is to really look at anger reactions and see them for what they are. Only then can we break free from this desperate and deadly disguise. The following chapter will look at a special group of people who, tragically, are unable to remove their anger masks: warriors for whom the war never ends.

CHAPTER 7

THE WARRIOR

Remember stories about King Arthur and the knights of the round table? These brave and gallant men were the "chosen few" selected to defend Arthur's kingdom from evildoers. When marauders threatened the kingdom they put on their armor, armed themselves with swords, cat-o'-nines, and shields, mounted their trusty steeds and prepared to battle to the death. Movies about medieval times are dramatic and exciting! Knights are portrayed as courageous and powerful "supermen." Yes, these men were brave and self-sacrificing. But what we forget is the tremendous pain and suffering that accompanies the glory of battle. Many were stabbed, beheaded with swords, gored with jousting spears, crushed with cat-o'-nines. Great numbers of men died, and those who survived rarely returned to their prebattle state of being. Although unscathed on the surface, many probably suffered from a mental illness, posttraumatic stress disorder (PTSD). This disorder results when an individual is subjected to such horrifying and overwhelming psychological trauma (such as killing and maiming others, fearing for one's own survival, and witnessing the deaths of one's comrades) they experience emotional overload. Although still perfectly "normal" looking on the outside, they are forever changed. Bouts of depression and anxiety become the norm. Sleep becomes a time of terror as nightmares about traumatic events invade their dreams. Noises that formerly caused no concern take on new meaning, sending them diving under chairs as they relive combat experiences. Plagued with doubts and fearful of further suffering, many withdraw from society, unable to form and maintain relationships, stay gainfully employed, and participate in society as other men do.

Sadly, Arthur's knights are not the only people affected by PTSD. Men from all wars suffer from the after effects of combat. Rape victims, survivors of natural disasters, child abuse, and sexual exploitation, rescue workers who witness the outcomes of terrible accidents, and medical professionals working in trauma units, emergency rooms, and intensive care units also experience lasting negative effects. These individuals "walk away" from their experiences physically intact but psychologically wounded. Stripped of their innocence, their values and beliefs about what is just and good are forever altered. Many hide their symptoms by assuming peripheral positions in family, social, and career settings. Carefully fabricating images of fitness so "no one will know" how damaged they really are.

My work in the trauma recovery program at the Houston Veterans Affairs Medical Center primarily involves intervention with combat survivors. Survivors of all traumas need our support and understanding; however, because my exposure to civilian trauma survivors is limited, this chapter is dedicated to "my veterans," the soldiers from World War II, the Korean War, the Vietnam War, and the Persian Gulf War. They served bravely, suffer greatly, and are for the most part, feared and misunderstood by the American public. Like all trauma survivors, they present a "socially acceptable image" to avoid compounding their trauma. Many are too damaged to work, plagued by memories of battles long since forgotten by the rest of us. They struggle to fit in, to be loved and accepted, and to control symptoms that threaten their sanity on a daily basis. Unlike other trauma survivors, their disguise is distinct: the mask of a warrior; a shield against the contempt of others and painful memories of acts committed in war. I hope reading this chapter will forever change your image of the combat veteran. These men are bright, sensitive, caring individuals who suffer greatly. They went into combat as innocent young boys and the horrors of war sent them back to us "changed men." Here is their story as I understand it.

When young men become soldiers they put on camouflage fatigues, combat boots, field packs, and weapons. They spend several grueling months in basic training, learning how to be warriors. Once this training ends, they go on to specialized training in a number of career fields. During peacetime they serve in a variety of settings and their jobs are much like any other job. This changes radically when war erupts. They are called upon to put into action the things learned in basic training. It is no longer a question of field exercises, this is for real. In training there are mock battles; casualties (both wounded and dead) get up at the end of the exercise deemed "whole and alive." In real war, soldiers cannot "undo" what has happened. People die, lose limbs, are terribly disfigured. They cry out for their mothers and friends as they lie dying from mortal wounds. Others, terrified and grief stricken, cradle their broken comrades in their arms, trying desperately to ease their pain and soothe their fears as they die. Combat medics, in filthy conditions with a bare minimum of supplies, try in vain to piece back together young men so damaged that even in the best of circumstances they could not survive.

Think how terrifying and shocking it would be to experience the death and destruction of war. Even as a "seasoned adult" of almost 40, I'm not sure I could get through it emotionally intact. Combat soldiers are *young*! Most are between 17 and 25 and have little knowledge of death and dying. Images of becoming heroes quickly fade when the glory of battle becomes the horror of war. Their beliefs about life, values learned from their families and religious leaders are shattered in a matter of minutes as they participate in combat. Kill or be killed, don't stop and think about the enemy as fellow human beings, just kill them! Don't stop and think about how you will feel when it's all over, just keep killing! Combat forever changes those involved. They must "forget" all they ever learned about humanity and fair play. The Ten Commandments no longer apply. They must learn to numb themselves against the terrible and unspeakable acts which they observe and commit in order to survive. Nobody tells them how to remember the rules of humanity and fair play, how to once again embrace the Ten Commandments when the war ends. What becomes of these young men when they return to the "free" world?

Returning from war is, in some instances, more traumatic than combat. Combat veterans from the Vietnam War are probably the most affected. The public viewed this war negatively and responded with strong sanctions against those who participated. These soldiers were in the jungle killing one day and home in civilian clothes the next, expected to "pick up where they left off" as if nothing had happened. Scorned by the public, called baby killers and murderers, they lived with then and continue to struggle now with the painful reality of what they were forced to participate in 30 years ago. Unable to share their memories with family members and friends, they withdrew in silence, suffering under the weight of their memories. Many, because they were so young, became "frozen in time," unable to move beyond their image as warriors. In combat they were respected and their actions had meaning. Once home they were hated and feared; so psychologically traumatized they could not identify much less carry out activities to create a sense of personal competence and purpose. I work with men in their late 40's and early 50's who still describe themselves as combat soldiers (present tense). They never moved beyond this role because they lost a piece of themselves and have never been able to find it. Innocence lost, dreams broken, values shattered, their lives were so upended they have never discovered the men behind the warrior mask. Afraid to look for fear of what they might find, they remain warriors on the outside and empty shells on the inside. The following stories, modified to protect the identity of the soldiers, will give you a greater appreciation for what these men experienced and why they must remain forever warriors.

Pregnant and Dying

Mr. P was a combat medic in Vietnam. His job was to stabilize wounded soldiers until they could be airlifted to field hospitals. He also cared for South Vietnamese civilians wounded during battles. One day Mr. P's platoon came upon a young Vietnamese woman who was about 8 months pregnant. She was mortally wounded and begged Mr. P to save her baby's life. He was about to perform a cesarean section but was ordered to let the baby die with the mother. When he challenged this order he was told, "If you attempt to save that baby, I will kill you." Mr. P was in his early 20's and very much wanted to survive, so he left the woman, with great difficulty, and moved forward with his platoon. Thirty years later he can still clearly recall the face of this young woman, the pain and anguish of knowing she was dying and her unborn child was doomed to die with her. He is haunted with this memory and has tremendous guilt for not disobeying orders and saving the child. Efforts to help him look at the situation in context have failed because he feels responsible for the death of that innocent unborn child. He remains trapped behind the mask of a warrior, because if he removed it and saw himself for what he is, a compassionate and caring person forced to make a terrible, irrevocable decision in wartime, he would have to face the terrible sadness in his life created by this event. How frightening to be trapped by a memory of such shocking proportions that the only way to remove your mask is to face and work through the painful feelings behind it. How would *you* feel having to walk away knowing a healthy unborn child would die as its mother died?

Mistaken Identity

Mr. Q, also a combat soldier in Vietnam, was on patrol one night. His squad was in a combat zone, aware that at any minute enemy soldiers might appear and start shooting. They moved cautiously, shielded by the darkness of the moonless night. Mr. Q became separated from the other soldiers and wandered into a no-fire zone near a local village. He was confused, not sure of his coordinates, so kept his guard up lest he be surprised by enemy troops. Suddenly, he heard a noise behind him. He turned, his weapon on full automatic, spraying bullets into the darkness. He later learned he had killed two young boys who had been out fishing. The grief generated by this horrible accident so scarred Mr. Q that he has lived for 28 years hating himself and his government for putting him in such a position. Unable to remember but let go, he remains a warrior on the outside and a broken man on the inside.

THE FAMILY

Mr. R was a helicopter gunner in Vietnam. He manned the machinegun on a helicopter and shot enemy soldiers from the air when ordered to do so by the pilot. One day his team was returning from a mission and saw a Vietnamese family crossing the field. There was a father and grandfather pulling a small wagon with a mother, two small children, and a handful of household possessions inside. Mr. R said it was very evident that this family was harmless so he took no action to impede their progress. His commanding officer ordered him to fire on the family. He tried to explain that they were innocent civilians and was told that if he did not obey the order he would be thrown from the helicopter to his death. He opened fire, killing the entire family. Mr. R was initially numb but as he realized what he had done, he became so distraught that he emotionally disintegrated. He described this experience as feeling like pieces of himself were falling off with every step he took. Mr. R continues, 28 years later, to relive this event in his mind. A kind and gentle man by nature, he has never forgiven himself for this event and cannot see it as an act committed under duress in the context of war. He can only see it as a terrible, unforgivable act of violence which, tragically, cannot be undone. He can still describe each family member so vividly I can see them in my mind. His grief is so fresh it brought tears to my eyes. He remains a warrior because he lost himself that day and has no clear sense of who he is or might become. The warrior is the only image he has to cling to. How would you react to such a memory that cannot be erased or forgotten?

CRAPS, YOU LOSE

Mr. S was assigned to a combat unit in Vietnam and spent months in the field. Using the bathroom meant going into the woods, and if lucky and near a field base, the outhouse. One day Mr. S started toward the outhouse closest to his position. Another soldier said, "Hey, I was about to go, why don't you use the other one?" The second outhouse stood about 50 yards further from their bunker. Mr. S responded, "Let's flip a coin and heads gets the closest toilet." Mr. S won the flip. The other soldier went to the far latrine and as he opened the door, it exploded. The soldier's leg was blown off and he later died. Mr. S lives with the terrible guilt that *he* killed this other soldier, that the booby trap was meant for him. Although this was a random act of warfare that Mr. S had no control over, he has lived for 30 years with survivor guilt. He continues to wear his warrior mask to avoid the painful reality that this event forever changed his life. In the warrior role he can claim, "It don't mean nothing" because this was a way to survive events in combat too horrible to think about. If he takes off the mask, he will be forced to face the fact that it *does* mean something. Then he must deal with the feelings this realization would release. Just imagine if you were involved in a coin toss and somebody died. How would you cope with being the survivor?

DEAD FRIENDS

Mr. RS was a "grunt" (front line infantryman) in the Vietnam War. His unit frequently participated in combat missions and a number of his friends were wounded and killed in action. One day the fighting was especially fierce. The members of the unit were separated, and once the fighting ended, two were discovered missing in action. The remaining members spent the next 2 days searching for their missing comrades. The morning of the third day they found them. The men had been tortured and killed. They had been decapitated, their heads placed on spears driven into the ground for all to see. The bodies had been mutilated and left for scavengers to eat. Mr. RS was assigned to collect body parts and place them in body bags so his friends could be shipped home for burial. He said the bodies had already begun to rot and the smell was putrid. The horror of collecting friends piece by piece is still with him, as are the smells from the decaying remains. Although this event happened 26 years ago, the images continue to haunt Mr. RS in nightmares and flashbacks. He can still see his mutilated friends, their faces frozen in silent screams of terror. He can still smell their rotting bodies, and feel his own fear of becoming the next victim. These images have trapped him in a warrior role because each time he attempts to remove the mask that conceals it, the horror of what he finds beneath frightens him into raising it once again. How would you cope with picking up the rotting pieces of your friends to send home to their grief-stricken families? How would you handle never being able to "tell your story" because it so horrified others they shut you down? You too might choose to keep wearing the mask of a warrior.

THE PROMISE

Mr. T had just celebrated his 18th birthday when he shipped out to Vietnam. He was placed in a combat unit and spent his first 3 months in the field. One day his company was attacked by enemy troops. One of the soldiers in his bunker, also about 18, was hit during a mortar attack. His legs were both severed and he lay bleeding to death. Mr. T frantically called for a medic, knowing his comrade was so damaged the medic would only ease his pain with morphine until he died. The young man began to cry, calling for his mother. He begged Mr. T not to let him die. Mr. T, attempting to provide comfort, cradled the soldier in his arms, gently holding him and promising him he would not die. His own agony was great because he knew in his heart this young man had no chance for survival. The soldier finally died and Mr. T helped place him in a body bag for the trip home. He still sees visions of this terrified young man, crying out for his mother and begging not to die. He remembers how helpless he felt, knowing this soldier would die, lying to ease his pain by telling him he wouldn't.

The wounded soldier died a teen, and Mr. T became frozen in late adolescence, unable to move beyond this horrible memory to continue his life. He wears the mask of a warrior because he is afraid if he confronts this memory head on he will die or go crazy. He was so young, so innocent. It wasn't fair for him to experience this degree of trauma at such a tender age. But war is not fair. It is brutal and ugly, destroying the lives of anyone and anything in its path. Just imagine if you were 18 years old and had to hold a terrified, mortally wounded peer in your arms until he died. You, too, might elect to wear the warrior mask to avoid looking at the horrifying trauma that lies just beneath the surface.

I share these stories not to shock you but to help you understand. When I think about all the categories of mental illness, I believe PTSD is the most difficult for laypeople to understand. Since this illness is not due to genetics or biochemical imbalances, people often think it cannot be a disease. Indeed, one of my veterans recently asked me, "How can you say PTSD is a mental illness? It happened to me because of something I experienced in war, not because I got sick." My response was that the trauma itself is not an illness. But the person's reactions across time are what result in mental illness. Some people experience trauma, work through it, and get back to "normal" life. Those unable to resolve trauma issues develop symptoms that interfere with their ability to participate, as they wish, in family, social, and employment settings. The longer the symptoms last, the more chronic the condition becomes. It is an illness because it drastically alters individuals' lives and prevents them from achieving their full potential. Another thing to remember when thinking about PTSD is that most individuals who have it look perfectly normal—until stressed. At that point they become aggressive or withdrawn, unable to effectively address and resolve the source of their distress. Much safer to keep up the warrior mask; it keeps others from getting close enough to see what lies beneath. This is, however, a deadly mask that gradually destroys its victims by keeping them from being real. Trapped in a role that demands imperviousness, they can never let down their guard and ask for the help so desperately needed. Remember this chapter when you cross paths with a former combat veteran or *any* trauma survivor. Your willingness to validate their pain may be the first step in helping them remove the warrior mask.

One final mask must be identified before moving on to look at the costs each mask generates for the wearer and those who love them: This is the ugly duckling mask. Individuals who wear this mask have a distorted view of themselves that prevents them from seeing their inner strength and beauty. For those with mental illnesses, this can be fatal. Failing to identify purpose or meaning in their lives, many choose death as an escape or withdraw into a secluded and lonely existence. Let's take a closer look at this special group of people.

CHAPTER 8

THE UGLY DUCKLING

Remember the story of the ugly duckling? The main character of this story is a baby swan reared by a family of ducks that has no idea he is really a swan. Awkward and unattractive he doesn't look at all like his brothers and sisters. The butt of cruel jokes and teasing, he comes to believe himself ugly. As time passes he is transformed into a beautiful swan. His family is amazed by this transition, as is he. This story has a happy ending: The swan, more beautiful than any other creature in the lake, is loved and admired by all who see him. Unfortunately, in real life, such is not always the case.

Human beings have an uncanny way of targeting those who are different and singling them out for derision. This can be especially devastating to those with mental illnesses. People may initially make fun of individuals with physical disabilities, but they usually reach a point of acceptance or benign indifference. After all, nobody wants to be missing a limb, wearing hearing aids, or using a wheelchair. We come to believe these "unfortunate" people should receive our support or at least not be stared at or ridiculed. The attitude toward those with mental disabilities is *very* different.

Since symptoms of mental illness are often invisible unless the person is very sick, they receive little or no support from others. Shunned for not "fitting in," they are frequently labeled "lazy," "unmotivated," and "unproductive." Over time this erodes their sense of self-worth making it difficult to justify a reason for continued existence. Failure to live up to society's definition of success (career, family, upward mobility), regardless of the reason, reinforces the notion that value is based on what one does rather that who one is. For those with mental illnesses this loss of capacity to participate fully in society becomes a greater handicap than their disability. An example will help you better understand the dramatic impact social attitudes have on an individual's self-image.

THE MISFIT

U, raised in an abusive family, was frequently told she was ugly, stupid, and worthless. She had an *unidentified* learning disability that made it difficult for her to perform well in school, and she received negative messages from her teachers and peers. At age 15 she was raped by a gang of high school youths. She went to her family and school officials for help and was told by her family, "It never happened, you're too ugly for somebody to rape." School officials asked her, "Do you have any witnesses? If not, there is nothing we can do." At this point U resigned herself to the fact that she was destined to a lifetime of abuse. She developed a mental condition called borderline personality disorder. People with this disorder have a poor self-image, often resort to self-destructive acts, and are unable to develop and maintain relationships and careers. U also suffers from major depression and a substance abuse disorder, further reducing her potential to live up to "the American dream."

By the time U reached her early 30's she had such a low opinion of herself she attempted suicide. Convinced she did not deserve to live, she slit both wrists. Fortunately, family members found her before it was too late. U, never married, has 2 children. She has never been able to hold a job for more than one or two months so she cannot support herself or her children. After years of struggling to give her children the best life possible, she came to the painful realization that she simply could not rear them in the type of environment she wanted them to grow up in. At great sacrifice to herself, she gave up both children for adoption. Until recently she lived with the same family members who physically, verbally, and emotionally abused her when she was a child.

When U feels bad about herself she bangs her head, cuts herself, burns her arms, and participates in other self-destructive acts (shoplifting, unprotected sex, drug abuse). Although this behavior is a desperate attempt to get others to see how sick and needy she is, it has the reverse effect: People are disgusted by what they see as manipulation and "bad acting." Even mental health professionals find U difficult to work with because she feels so unworthy she repeatedly sabotages efforts of help.

As you can see, U is a very sick woman. Unfortunately for U, she *looks* perfectly normal. Unless she is acting out nobody would know she is ill. She cannot work but is ineligible for disability benefits because: (1) she receives family support; (2) she is young; and (3) in the eyes of officials controlling disability funds she has not gotten "sick enough" to merit compensation. She was unable to raise her children, but instead of receiving sympathy faces scorn and contempt from those who believe she could pull her life together if she really tried. Dependent on the family that abused her for her basic survival needs, U continues to receive constant feedback about what a failure her whole life has been. So what will become of this very sick woman?

This client has been the challenge of my career! Initial efforts to place her in safe housing and establish financial support were repeatedly sabotaged. Every plan I developed, U systematically dismantled. This became so frustrating that I pleaded for the help of my supervisor and professional peers. After addressing my own negative reactions to U's behavior, I was able to provide ongoing support, constructively confront her self-destructive behavior, and invite her to consider more productive options. U has come a long way in the 2 years I have known

her. She finally removed herself from destructive family relationships and now lives in a halfway house that offers support
and encouragement. She has applied for financial assistance
and is prepared to deal with the fact that receiving disability
benefits will be a long and uphill battle. She attends therapy
sessions faithfully, is attempting to stay drug and alcohol free,
and asks for help when she feels self-destructive instead of acting on impulses as she did in the past.

U may never hold a job and it is doubtful, if she has more
children, that she will ever be well enough to raise them. She
is, however, learning to identify her worth in terms of who she
is inside rather than by society's standards, which in her case,
are totally unrealistic. Think of all the people like U who never
get the help they need. Even with help, living with mental disorders as disabling as U's is difficult. Without intervention, many
such people die or live marginal lives filled with emotional pain
and isolation. Let's look at some analogies to further illustrate
how painful it can become to live behind the mask of an ugly
duckling.

The Warthog

When I was a little girl my body was covered with thousands of
tiny warts. My mouth, hands, and knees were the most affected
and I was very self-conscious about these unsightly blemishes.
To make matters worse, my peers referred to me as "the wart
hog." As time passed I began to avoid my peers and "hid" my
hands and knees when I had to be around others. Unfortunately, I could not hide my mouth so the teasing continued.
When I was older a dermatologist removed most of my warts
with liquid nitrogen. I was relieved to be free of my "wart hog"
image but continued to feel bad about myself for a long time.
The years of teasing had done their damage and I never felt as
pretty as other girls. As I reached my early 30's (yes, it took
that long!) the revelation that beauty is only skin deep finally

sunk in. I began to focus instead on my inner strengths and others responded positively. As time passed, my acceptance of myself as "okay just the way you are" led to changes on many levels. I became friendlier and more self-confident, my looks improved because I felt better about myself; I developed a sense of humor. When I look back at that pitiful little girl I am amazed by how far I have come. Luckily for me I had a loving family, a basically sound mind and body, and a willingness to face my greatest fears (rejection and social disapproval). What of those less fortunate?

Many individuals with mental illnesses are teased and ridiculed for being different. The harder they try to fit in, the more it magnifies how different they are. Struggling to be "like everybody else," they sacrifice a little bit more of themselves each day. Unlike me, they cannot go to the dermatologist (or any other doctor for that matter) and have their blemishes removed. Medication helps manage the symptoms of mental illness but it does not cure or make those affected forget about their disability. Since others cannot see their pain, they must endure ongoing criticism and thoughtless questions like "Why don't you work? You look pretty healthy to me"; "Why are you acting so weird?"; "Why can't you be more like the rest of us?"; "What's the matter with you?"; "You just aren't trying hard enough"; "Doesn't it bother you that your spouse/parents are supporting you?"; "If you were really sick I could understand, but a mental illness, come on!" How would *you* feel if you had a disabling condition that was treatable but not curable? How would you feel if others could not see what you felt like on the inside so kept prodding you to get on with it. Think about how, over time, you might begin to question whether you really are sick, and how this would affect your self-esteem and relationships with others.

BIRD LEGS

Before my middle sister died there were three girls in my family. My oldest sister and I were graced with very muscular legs. My middle sister inherited slender legs. I always lamented the fact that my legs were built like tree trunks and my middle sister fussed about her slender legs. My oldest sister's legs were in between the two and she was apparently happy with hers. My middle sister, highly sensitive to criticism, was mortified when peers referred to her as "bird legs." This negative image frequently reduced her to tears. As she got older, she avoided wearing shorts to reduce the risk of being called bird legs. Years passed and we all forgot about the "bird legs" comments until one day, in her late 30's, she wore shorts, and an unsuspecting guest said, "Your legs are so slender, they're just like bird legs." Well, you can imagine her response—she was humiliated. She never let on how much this comment hurt her but reverted back to wearing long pants even during the hottest of Texas summers. Although "bird leg" comments were very troubling to my sister, people's reactions to her mental illness created far worse results.

Linda once told me she realized something was wrong emotionally when she was in her late teens. She was anxious a lot and struggled to keep herself from "freaking out." She said work was always difficult because she had to act like everything was fine even when she thought she would scream. As she aged, her symptoms worsened. Depression became a wet, heavy blanket she struggled to throw off each morning when she awoke. The accompanying anxiety and identity confusion she experienced drove her to "self-medicate" symptoms with both prescription and illicit drugs. As her addiction grew, so did her mental illness. It became more and more difficult for her to hide symptoms. We all knew something was wrong but it was only a few years before her death that we discovered she was mentally ill. My sister felt deep shame about her mental illness. Her perception of herself as an "ugly duckling" in a pond full of swans contributed to her tragic death. If only she could have seen her inner beauty, and drawn on it to compensate for her limitations. She, like thousands of others, was unable to make this connection which, sadly, extracts the ultimate price—life.

Think how you might react if you felt so worthless, so hopelessly damaged that life became more of a burden than a gift, *knowing* that you might never get better and would, in all likelihood, probably get worse. How would you cope with an ugly duckling image that you weren't quite sure how to remove? What steps would *you* take that would lead you to discover the beauty lying just beneath the surface of your disability that others can see so clearly? Do you think you could meet this challenge or might you end up like my sister in a downward spiral that could only end in death?

IGNORANCE CAN BE DEADLY

When I was about 12 I had a good friend named Dale. Unfortunately, Dale suffered from asthma and had regular nosebleeds, so people were always laughing at him. Being sickly, he was small for his age, and the fact that his older brother was one of the finest looking guys in school didn't help matters any. Dale amazed me because he always had such a positive attitude. Once I asked him how he managed all those comments without letting them affect him. He responded, "Oh, they hurt all right, but I have realized people are just ignorant. They have no idea how bad it makes me feel or they wouldn't do it. I hope they never have to find out just how hard being different really is." As you can see, Dale had a really good heart. I was never so gracious when being teased about my warts! Even at his young age Dale realized that unless people have been affected by something, or know someone who has, they have no comprehension of and little sympathy for what they don't understand.

I can relate to Dale's story through the premature birth of my son. Just a year before my son's birth a good friend had experienced the premature birth of twins. She was hospitalized for a month before their birth in an attempt to forestall the inevitable. I visited her during this ordeal, showing concern and love, never knowing how devastating this experience really was—*until* I faced it myself the following year. I watched my tiny baby attached to all sorts of equipment, silenced by ventilator tubes, blinded by eye pads to protect his immature vision, in constant pain from the life-saving measures being applied with no guarantee of survival and only guesses about how damaged he might be *if* he survived. Only when it was *my* baby did I *really* know how terrible premature birth can be.

My son was in the neonatal intensive care unit for 4 months. As time passed, I saw new parents come in, devastated and in shock. I knew how they felt and tried to offer support and comfort. When I see pregnant women I always say a silent prayer that they have a long and healthy pregnancy. When I hear someone wish for an early delivery I fight back the urge to say, "My God! Be grateful you're so pregnant! You don't know what you are asking for!" Yes, experience is the best teacher of compassion and humility. I hope this book will serve a similar purpose because I would not wish the pain of mental illness on anyone.

My experience with my sister's mental illness was even worse than watching my premature son struggle for survival. Seeing her disintegrate over a period of 6 years was devastating. Each hospitalization was more traumatic, each suicide attempt more upsetting than the last. Knowing that someday, like a marked beast, she would die and nothing I could do would change the course of her illness. No professional connections, political strings, or personal favors could help. Love, encouragement, and prayer only delayed the inevitable. Linda was destined to die because the society in which she lived does not believe how serious and widespread this problem really is. Treatment for mental illness, if the affected person is willing to face the stigma of admitting they have a mental disorder, is beyond the financial reach of most Americans. Insurance companies provide limited coverage, private funds are quickly exhausted, free beds are few and sought after by many, state institutions are dangerously understaffed with waiting lists so long that many die before they can be admitted.

Those who suffer reach a point where they have no more energy to cope. The pain of living becomes so intense that even the thought of how hurt their families will be if they kill themselves fades away. The pain is so intense that the only option is death. I tell you this hoping you can gain "a sense of" because I hope you will *never* experience the pain of being a passive participant in the gradual and unalterable process of watching someone you love die an inch at a time. I hope you will never see a loved one become a shadow of themselves until the shell finally collapses from the weight of the pain it has endured and they slip silently from this world into the next. Yes, the ugly duckling mask extracts a high cost from those who wear it. They never feel "as good as," never believe they can "live up to," others' expectations. They never know how it feels to wake up and feel "normal," at peace with oneself.

THE MIRROR

Have you ever walked through the fun house of a carnival? It is filled with all manner of sights and sounds to distort our perception of reality. The most exciting part for me is the hall of mirrors. In this room, all things become possible. The short become tall, the fat become thin, the beautiful become grotesque, and vice versa. Images are so distorted that if you stayed in the fun house for any length of time you would begin to question your dimensions! Luckily the hall of mirrors is simply an illusion and once you leave, life reverts back to "normal time." For better or for worse you go back to being who you were before you entered. What if you were forever doomed to assume the dimensions assigned to you in the hall of mirrors? If once you left, you were forever frozen in the form of the last mirror you gazed into? It would be wonderful if you came out tall, thin, and beautiful. But what if you came out short, fat, and disfigured? How horrifying to have such a fun event turn into an episode of *Night Gallery!*

Many individuals with mental illnesses experience a similar and very real fate. Trapped inside minds that have short-circuited, and painfully aware of the fact that something is terribly wrong, they struggle to assume "normal dimensions" even when this costs them their dignity, self-esteem, and in some cases, their lives. Desperate to be accepted, they resort to extreme measures to cover up flaws they fear others might not understand. Since their "ugly duckling" lives within, others do not notice that they perceive themselves as "damaged goods." Unable to identify and mobilize their strengths and talents, they silently slip down the well toward the slimy water below. There is no rope to pull them up (because nobody knows they are slipping), no footholds to slow their descent, no one to hear their calls for help (because they're screaming on the inside). The lower they sink, the more convinced they become that the world would be a better place if they departed, that their families would suffer less if they ceased to exist. Unlike the swan who grows from homeliness to beauty, these individuals *perceive* themselves to be growing in the opposite direction. Beliefs become reality, and in their minds they become more of a liability with each passing day. Trapped in a permanent hall of mirrors, they lose all sight of their true identities. Perceiving themselves to be so damaged that there is no hope for repair they withdraw or die.

We have now come to a turning point in this book. The last six chapters have been devoted to exploring masks worn by mentally ill individuals in their desperate attempt to "fit in" and "be normal." I have identified six of the most common masks I have seen in my 10 years as a psychiatric social worker. There are many variations of these masks, and, to further complicate matters, individuals often wear more than one mask depending on where they are, whom they are with, and what is going on in their lives. This makes it much more difficult to recognize individuals living behind masks so they can be encouraged to remove them.

Costumes are fun if they are associated with events like Halloween (school carnivals, trick-or-treat, and neighborhood parties), Mardi Gras (when people from all over descend on New Orleans, Louisiana, for a little fun and frivolity), or Fasching (a German holiday where people dress up and party in the streets). What of costumes that are worn out of grim determination to avoid disclosure of one's true self? These masks are *not* fun, they are deadly! You have seen the extreme costs of this behavior in terms of emotional pain and premature death in the stories I have shared thus far. In the next chapter we will explore these costs more intimately before going on to explore why, if the cost of wearing these masks is so high, people continue to wear them.

CHAPTER 9

THE PRICE WE ALL PAY

What price does wearing a mask to hide the symptoms of mental illness extract from us as individuals, families, and members of society? Does a price tag exist that accurately reflects the intense emotional agony experienced by patients, the mental anguish of family members, the stress generated because those affected cannot participate fully in society? Indeed, there is not enough money in the world to compensate for the personal suffering that results when people live their lives under cover to avoid the stigma attached to the label "mental illness." In chapter 2 I introduced information describing how widespread and serious mental illness is. These statistics highlighted the number of *identified* cases (many are never identified because they fail to seek help), the most common types of mental illness, and the impact of mental illness on children, the elderly, and those with AIDS. These statistics provided startling information about homelessness, mentally ill individuals jailed without criminal charges, and deaths from suicide. Before further discussing these *personal* costs of mental illness, I want to briefly address the economic costs that result as individuals struggle to appear normal; to live up to the American dream. The following statistics provide an overview of expenditures in terms of dollars and cents:

• Mental illnesses impose a multibillion dollar burden on the economy each year. Total economic costs amounted to $147.8

billion in 1990. More than 31% of those costs, $46.6 billion, are for anxiety disorders (*The Economic Burden of Affective Disorders*, Dorothy P. Rice, Sc.D., and Leonard S. Miller, Ph.D., 1993).

- Direct cost—expenditures for professional health care for persons suffering from mental disorders, including care in mental specialty institutions, hospitals, and nursing homes, physician and other professional services, and prescription drugs—accounted for $67 billion, or 11.4% of all personal health care expenditures in 1990 (Rice and Miller, 1993).

- Three independent studies between 1971 and 1985 found that mental health costs remained relatively constant during the past 20 years, ranging from 9 to 11% of direct costs for health care (Bazelon Center for Mental Health Law, 1993).

- Direct treatment and support costs comprised 45.3% of the total economic costs of mental disorders. The value of reduced or lost productivity comprised 42.7% of the total economic costs of mental disorders. Mortality costs comprise 8%, and other related costs, including expenditure for criminal justice, the value for caregiver services, comprise 4% percent (Rice and Miller, 1993).

- Morbidity costs—the value of goods and services not produced because of mental disorders—amounted to $63.1 billion for all mental disorders in 1990. Morbidity costs for anxiety disorders account for $34.2 billion; for schizophrenia, $10.7 billion. The morbidity costs for anxiety disorders reflect their prevalence in the population and the high rate of lost productivity (Rice and Miller, 1993).

- Mortality costs—the current value of lifetime earnings lost by all who died in 1990 because of mental disorders—amounted to $11.8 billion in 1990 (Rice and Miller, 1993).

- Other relative costs—the costs indirectly related to the treatment and lost productivity of people with mental disorders—amounted to $6 billion in 1990 (Rice and Miller, 1993).

- The mental health system relies on a high proportion of funds from public sources rather than private insurance and

Source: The above statistics are from the Mental Health Information Center, National Mental Health Association, Alexandria, Virginia. For further information on these statistics, contact: Office of External Liaison, Center of Mental Health Services, 5600 Fishers Lane, Room 13-103, Rockville, Maryland 20857; telephone (301) 443-2792.

out-of-pocket payments. In 1990, 28% of funds for mental health care came from state and local governments. In general health care, the comparable figure was 14%. Medicare, Medicaid, VA, and other federal programs accounted for an additional 26% (National Advisory Mental Health Council).

As you can see we lose billions of dollars each year as a result of mental illness. What of the *personal* expense imposed on affected individuals and those they love? The best place to begin is with the fears and frustrations of patients and family members. The following are remarks I have encountered during my career in psychiatry. Listen carefully to the message each imparts. You cannot help but hear the desperation, the hopelessness, the utter despair that results from having or living with mental illness, especially for those unable to take off their masks.

> What did we do wrong? Why did *our* child develop schizophrenia?
> How can I come to terms with this, knowing I can never be what I dreamed about all my life?
> Who will take me seriously if they find out I'm mentally ill?
> What will happen to our child when we die? Who will take care of him or her?
> We ran out of money for private psychiatric care and _____ killed him- or herself before the state institution could free up a bed. Why can't people understand how desperately we need more affordable mental health care? Why did _____ have to die?"
> If you could see the pain in my child's eyes, you would pray for blindness. It is so painful watching someone you love suffer knowing you can't make their pain stop.
> I watched my sister mouth the words "Please let me die" around her ventilator tube after a suicide attempt. I can't imagine being in such pain that the only escape is death.
> The voices torment me to the point where I want to rip my head open and pull them out. Even with medication the most I can hope for is to turn them down.
> What kind of life do I have ahead of me? I'm only 28.

When I get manic I go kinda crazy. I never know what to expect next. It's like fast forwarding a videotape but there's no stop button. Your thoughts just race ahead carrying you with them whether you like it or not.

Can you imagine being in *my* shoes—when just staying alive is such a struggle? Forget about quality of life—there isn't any.

A lot of people commit suicide. Someday I might be one of them. I'm glad I can't see into the future, I'm afraid of what I might find.

I look into the faces of my family and see their pain and confusion. How can I possibly help them understand that this is the real deal, I'm not just play acting?

The hardest part of having a mental illness is not being taken seriously. Sometimes I feel as if I have on an invisible cloak and nobody sees me. It's as if I'm already dead but my heart hasn't gotten the message to stop beating.

If there's no cure for this, what's the point of continuing? My life has been a living hell since I got sick. I'd rather be dead than live like I am now.

I am an empty shell. There is no joy in my life.

Sometimes I wish I could jump out of my skin and into someone else's. Then I think who do I hate badly enough to make them take my place, and I can never come up with *anyone* I hate that much.

I had such hope for the future. Now I only see darkness. The American dream just died and took me with it.

What a double bind. People tell you to get out there and live your life but everywhere you go there's a roadblock. Yeah, the Americans with Disabilities Act is great on paper, but people find ways to get around it. I might as well have a sign around my neck saying, "Mentally ill, stay back 50 feet to avoid injury."

Mental illness is a lot like having AIDS, everyone is afraid of you, they think you did something to bring it on yourself, and they hope that if they just don't look at it somehow it will miraculously disappear. I used to think like that too—until I became *one of them.* It's amazing how life changes when it's *you* who's in the barrel!

We're tried everything and nothing works, now what do we do?

These are statements made by patients and family members struggling to come to grips with the fact that mental illness lasts a lifetime. At this writing there are no known cures. We have come a long way in the last 100 years but psychiatry is still a new science and not nearly as predictable as mathematics or physics. With mental illness there are no absolutes, and this makes treatment infinitely harder. How do you explain to someone trying to understand their illness that there are no rules that apply in all cases? That even if they follow treatment recommendations to the letter there are no guarantees, and that the best you can provide is an educated guess about possible long-range outcomes?

The costs to patients and their family members comes in the day-to-day worries about what the future might bring. There is, for example, the fear of saying or doing something that "triggers" an episode or upsets a family member. There is the concern that what you say or do might be used against you or someone you love. You live with the constant fear of discovery, and those with mental illnesses often choose to wear masks rather than become real because it's less complicated. For many, the cost of becoming real, as you'll see in a later chapter, is too great. At least while wearing masks they can maintain a facade of normalcy until someone gets a little too close and the image begins to fade. Let's look at some examples to help you get a better sense of what I'm saying.

MY BROTHER, MY SON

Mr. V was a 45-year-old man with a diagnosis of major depression and chronic substance abuse. I first met him in an outpatient substance abuse program 5 years ago. His parents were both dead, he had never married, and had no children. What Mr. V did have was a brother 15 years his senior who was very concerned about his well-being and who had stepped into the "father" role. Mr. V was living with his brother, not working, and using drugs on a regular basis to in his own words "stabilize my depression." The brother and his wife were at their wits'

end but did not know what to do. They felt if they "abandoned" Mr. V and he died it would be their fault. If they continued to support him and he died, it would also be their fault.
Mr. V had become very comfortable living with his brother and
had no intention of seeking recovery or employment though
he was still able to work. He had his family over a barrel and
only came into treatment on threat of eviction. Mr. V used the
ugly duckling mask to convince himself and family members
that he simply could not make it on his own and that illicit
drugs were the only way he could cope with his depression.

   This family's challenge is faced by millions of people with
mentally ill family members: How does one learn to identify
the fine line between helping and enabling before it's too late?
How can the family help the affected member identify and
draw on strengths instead of focusing on weaknesses? Part of
the work I did with this family was to help them distinguish
between temporary need versus chronic dependence. In times
of crisis we all need a helping hand but once the crisis is resolved, we pick ourselves up and go on—right? Ideally this is
what happens, but in many cases family members get confused
and keep on helping, often to the patient's detriment. The
longer one remains in a dependent role, the harder it is to
once again assume personal responsibility for our own lives.
This is true for *all* people not just those with identified mental
illnesses! So what's a family to do?

   The costs of "playing the game" (buying into the patient's
belief that he was incompetent and helpless) were emotional
anguish for the brother and his wife, increasing dependence
of the patient on his family, continuation of the addiction (why
stop if I don't have to?). Mr. V's depressive symptoms increased
(how could Mr. V get better when he was constantly altering
his brain chemistry with illicit drugs?). The final cost is guilt
on the family member's part if anything, and I mean *anything*
happens to Mr. V. The costs of ending the game and establishing new ground rules (helping Mr. V locate strengths hidden
behind his ugly duckling mask) are a temporary increase in

anxiety for everyone during the process of transition, along with the possibility that the patient will become more *or less* responsible if he has to accept consequences for his actions. The brother and his wife have an identified time limit for helping and then "get their lives back" (which does not mean they can no longer help but the type and amount of help must be modified). The patient develops a sense of personal competence and his self-esteem improves (hey, maybe I *can* take care of myself with careful planning). As you can see, the costs for continuing to help beyond normal limits can contribute to rather than alleviate symptoms of his mental illness (his depression worsens and his addiction remains active). This reinforces his ugly duckling image (I really am a lost cause). We will spend considerable energy in a later chapter addressing strategies for change.

IF I DIE BEFORE I WAKE

Mr. W was a 50-year-old man with a long history of alcoholism. He came into treatment at his parents' request. They were both 80 and in poor health. The primary issue presented during treatment was the parents' concern about what would happen to their son once they died. He had always lived at home, was unemployed, drank daily, and berated his parents at the slightest hint he should change his behavior. The crisis that brought this family into treatment was an episode of alcohol poisoning—Mr. W got into a chug-a-lug contest with a man half his age and almost died. After he was detoxified, Mr. W, at his parents' insistence, enrolled in an outpatient substance abuse clinic.

Mr. W was an expert at wearing the porcupine mask lest others see how truly insecure he was. After all, he had worn it since adolescence and the thought of "getting real" was too terrifying to consider. During treatment, attempts were made to have him think about how his life might look after his parents' deaths. Remarks of this nature were met with open displays of hostility and comments like, "What the hell are you trying to do, scare them into early graves?" This patient was simply too terrified to imagine life without his parents. He had never tested his wings, and over the years became skilled at using his porcupine mask to maintain the status quo. A major breakthrough for this family was when the parents *finally* realized they were killing their son with kindness, that if they continued to allow him to forego the consequences of his behavior until their deaths he would be left alone to face the harshness of the world with no skills and no support.

During a very intense session Mr. W took down his mask and showed his parents the little boy who had never grown up and didn't know how to be a man. This was the beginning of a long and difficult recovery. The cost: emotional pain, guilt, confusion and fear. The gains: opportunities for individual and personal growth, limit setting, reality testing, and improved family relationships. Mr. W did continue to live at home but with new rules which included: no drinking or drug use, participation in a family group to improve family communication, and the stipulation that Mr. W must seek job counseling and begin looking for work within 3 months. The long-term goal was for him to be living independently with family support within one year.

Mr. W achieved this goal and it was the proudest day of his life when he reported he was employed and had an apartment picked out. Was life happily ever after for Mr. W after he removed his porcupine mask? Of course not, this is *real life* not the movies! He did, however, discover parts of himself he could never find while wearing his mask. He also developed a deeper appreciation for his parents and began making efforts to give something back. Had he continued to wear his mask, he would most likely have met with a premature end to a very unhappy life. Now he has a chance at happiness and his parents, nearing the end of their lives, can die with the knowledge they helped prepare their son for life after they are gone. Let's look at one final example before moving on.

I'm So Happy I Could Just Die

Mr. X was a middle-aged man with a long history of major depression. Through the years he used work to cope with the symptoms of his illness and when asked, "How's it going" always responded "Just great!" Mr. X's marriage was approaching its 25th year. He had three teenage children, a full-time job, and an array of material possessions. On the outside he "looked" like the picture of health. Unfortunately for Mr. X, he often struggled with suicidal thoughts but was afraid to tell anyone for fear of being labeled "mentally ill" and locked away in a "psycho ward." Time passed and Mr. X, entering his late 40's experienced a midlife crisis. Feeling as if his youth were fading and his opportunities for advancement becoming increasingly limited, he started sleeping 12 to 18 hours a day, lost 35 pounds in 3 months, and was irritable with family members. Things got so bad at home his wife threatened to leave unless he sought help.

I met Mr. X during a psychiatric evaluation to determine how he might best be helped. A psychiatrist, psychologist, physician's assistant, and myself were involved in this interview along with the patient and his wife. He worked very hard to present an image of mental health and when asked if he ever had suicidal thoughts replied, "Of course not, do you think I'm crazy!" There was no hint of active suicidal thoughts or plans so hospitalization was not considered. He agreed to attend a weekly outpatient therapy group to address midlife issues and was to begin the following week. When Mr. X failed to attend his first group I called to see what had prevented his attendance. His wife answered the phone and said, "Don't you know? X went out in the backyard Saturday night and blew his brains out while the children and I were at the movies. He left a note saying he couldn't take it anymore and had decided to kill himself outside so he wouldn't make a mess of the house." This information stunned me. I, along with three other mental health professionals, had seen him less than a week before his death. There were no outward signs of suicidal intent and no way to predict this tragic outcome. Even his wife stated she had no idea he was so depressed and that he had cheerfully walked them to the door as they left for the movies saying, "Have a good time, I'll see you when you get back."

This is a true and shocking account of what can happen when a person hides symptoms behind a mask. The effort of keeping the masquerade going eventually becomes too much. Tragically, many, like Mr. X, kill themselves rather than admit that they have a mental illness. If Mr. X had identified his suicidal thoughts and plans we could have temporarily hospitalized him until the crisis passed. This would have allowed time for the antidepressant medication to work and for group therapy to provide a supportive environment for him to discuss his strong, negative feelings. Sadly for Mr. X and his family, he failed to understand that his crisis was time limited, that with help he could lead a fairly normal life. In this case, maintaining the picture of health cost Mr. X his life and left his family with a lifetime of "if only's" and "why's."

As you can see, wearing masks to cloak symptoms of mental illness can be deadly. Why then do people continue to wear them? What factors could possibly convince them to maintain this facade when it is dragging them toward their own deaths? What barriers are they so afraid to jump that they choose misery, isolation, or death over change? This is the focus of chapter 10.

CHAPTER 10

BARRIERS TO CHANGE

The facts, figures, and stories shared in chapters 1 to 9 taught you that wearing masks to disguise symptoms of mental illness is destructive, and in some cases fatal. Despite this truth many of us justify their continued use by rationalizing, "I have to wear a mask—it protects me from the painful reality of who I *really* am." Unfortunately, we fail to consider that the same mask keeping us safe also creates barriers that prevent us from seeking help when it is most desperately needed. Sacrificing ourselves emotionally to create images we think others want to see distorts our self-image, cripples our self-esteem, damages relationships, and impedes recovery. Originally worn to preserve and protect, masks gradually rob the wearer of their true identity. Like a person who continues adding layers of clothing to keep warm as the temperature drops, those wearing masks must continuously reinforce their disguise as others begin to see through it. The longer this process continues the more permanent becomes the mask, with each layer further distorting the image of the individual trapped beneath. Finally, so many layers are added that the individual's true identity is lost. This creates a crisis that, unless interrupted, produces highly undesirable consequences (worsening of symptoms, family conflict, social isolation, confusion about the meaning and purpose of one's continued existence, death).

Why then, if wearing masks is so costly, do we fiercely defend their continued use? Several factors play a role in this self-destructive process:

1. Negative social attitudes about mental illness.
2. Fear of rejection/abandonment.
3. The absence of effective coping skills.
4. Exhaustion.
5. Learned helplessness.

These factors condemn many to lives of isolation and misery. Negative social attitudes about mental illness "teach us" that being real often generates prejudice instead of understanding and acceptance. Ignorance about psychiatric illness, both among patients and the general population, breeds apprehension. Skepticism that mental illness is real illness since it cannot be seen or touched prevents us from seeking information to ease our doubts. Because we often lack effective coping skills to fight the dragon once it is recognized we avoid the hunt. Exhaustion from the constant struggle both without and within creates apathy and hopelessness. Learned helplessness, coming to believe that no matter what action is taken the result will always be the same, dooms us to inaction. A closer look at these factors will help you better understand the role they play in this deadly game of cat and mouse.

NEGATIVE SOCIAL ATTITUDES ABOUT MENTAL ILLNESS

This factor was discussed at length in chapter 1 so I invite you to reread that chapter. Suffice it to say that as a society we avoid the unfamiliar and when unable to do so, develop defensive reactions to reduce our anxiety. We secretly hope issues that create discomfort, if ignored long enough, will simply go away. Like small children afraid of monsters in the closet we lie huddled in fright when a quick flick of the light switch and a walk through the closet could dispel our fears. Our resistance to challenging existing social attitudes and exploring issues we don't understand prevents those with mental illnesses from successfully participating in mainstream America. Painfully aware of our discomfort they raise their masks, at great personal sacrifice, to help *us* feel more secure. Like a deaf person in a room full of hearing people, they "blend in" as best they can. Uncomfortable with their differences we rationalize, " *They* are the ones who are different. If they can't fit into our world it's *their* problem. It's just easier to ignore them than to try and understand." Let's look at the price tag this barrier creates.

THE ENGINEER

Mr. Y is a locomotive engineer I mentioned earlier, who has been employed by the same railroad for the past 15 years. Unfortunately, Mr. Y suffers from major depression. He has managed to mask his symptoms by staying focused on his work and avoiding others when off duty. Mr. Y, now 48, reports that his symptoms have gotten worse with each passing year since he turned 40. He has frequent crying spells, is unable to sleep more than 3 to 4 hours nightly, and feels so hopeless that at times he thinks about suicide. Mr. Y is willing to accept help, *however*, his railroad does regular urine tests to identify individuals who use drugs and alcohol. He is afraid of using antidepressant medication because when his urine tests positive, he will have to explain why the drugs they find are in his system. We assured Mr. Y that his psychiatrist will be more than happy to write a letter explaining why his medication is needed and identifying these medications as "safe" while operating machinery. His response: "Yeah, I know you would do that but I've seen what happened to several other people at the station. They told the boss they had psychiatric problems and needed medication to stabilize symptoms and eventually lost their jobs. I know the Americans with Disabilities Act states this is against the law but they find ways around it. First, you get the worst shift and the routes that *nobody* wants. They constantly check up on you to make sure you don't "get whacked out" and kill somebody. Going to work becomes so miserable and stressful you finally quit. I know you mean well but I can't afford to lose my job."

I can hear you now: "That's not fair! How can the railroad get away with such discrimination! There must be something Mr. Y can do!" Yes, he can file a grievance against the railroad but this singles him out as a "troublemaker" creating just as much tension as identifying his mental illness and having his urine be positive for antidepressant medication. The social attitude that people with mental illnesses, *especially* those who need medication, should *never* be allowed in "critical positions" is ignorant and narrow minded. Most individuals with mental illnesses are *very* aware of their limitations and will sacrifice jobs they really want if they think, even for a second, that they might otherwise harm others. Mr. Y could easily perform his current job with no more risk than his nonmedicated peers. Unfortunately, the fear of losing his job, based on what has happened to several of his peers, prevents him from accepting medication that could drastically improve the quality of his life. Ironically, medication would *improve* rather than impede his job performance by reducing symptoms of his depression. How sad to be forced to chose between your livelihood and your mental health! Kind of like being asked if you would rather die or be paralyzed. Such black-and-white thinking dramatically limits options for those who, in spite of disabling conditions, are sincerely attempting to make their way in this world.

The Maze Without End

Individuals with mental illnesses who apply for disability payments from state and federal agencies face an overwhelming, tedious, esteem-stomping experience that can last from 1 to 3 years. Like rape victims they must "prove" themselves deserving of their fellow citizens' support. They must identify their past work history, disclosing the painful and humiliating reasons why, time after time, they quit or were fired. Many have held 50 to 100 jobs over a 20-year span and for most, the longest job lasted only 3 to 6 months. They must produce documents from psychiatrists, psychologists, and vocational specialists that label them "unemployable," with detailed descriptions of their disabling condition and the limitations it creates. Telephone interviews, complicated forms, face-to-face interviews, and examinations are part of this difficult process. Since individuals with mental illnesses "look" normal large numbers have no hope of receiving disability payments even if they are very sick and have the documentation to prove it. Having the "right diagnosis" is critical, and in the days of managed care and "right sizing" many who genuinely deserve our support are deemed "ineligible."

Feeling abandoned and ashamed many give up, unable to go through the humiliation of appealing a negative determination. Some end up homeless, others rely on relatives for support. Sadly some die, casualties of a society that refuses to believe some individuals are just too sick to work. How frustrating to *know*, having tried and failed multiple times, that you cannot sustain a job across time. How appalling to realize that asking for help will generate skepticism and disgust in those who process your claim. How challenging to try and push past the shame and humiliation of having to *prove* oneself "less able" than other members of society. Yes, a change in social attitudes is long overdue so our more challenged members can enjoy the same rights and comforts the rest of us take for granted.

FEAR OF REJECTION/ABANDONMENT

Spawned by negative social attitudes about mental illness this factor leads individuals with psychiatric disabilities to hide and deny symptoms. All too often painful experiences in which others shy away from or criticize them once their diagnosis is known teaches affected individuals to mask this facet of their lives. My patients, struggling to come to terms with their differences, often ask the painful question, "Jo, how will I ever find someone to love me? Once they find out I have a mental illness they'll be gone. I know because I've had it happen before. Even though I am lonely I have resigned myself to the fact that nobody wants to deal with damaged goods." I generally respond with an analogy about sexually transmitted diseases (STD's).

"If I was HIV positive, I would not walk up to a potential partner and say hi I'm Jo and I am HIV positive! I would get to know the person and develop a relationship with them. Only after we had gotten to know one another would I begin to tell the more intimate details of my life, in this case, before the first sexual encounter. By waiting for the person to know *me* the chances of rejection, although still very real, would be lessened. If this person had come to love me, they might be willing to do the things necessary to have a sexual relationship with me while at the same time protecting themselves from contracting HIV. If I tell them I am HIV positive when we first meet there is no relationship so nothing for them to lose by walking away." Yes, it is challenging and at times painful, but when and how you disclose information about disabling conditions plays a big role in the way others respond. Let's look at an example.

LEARNING BOUNDARIES

My husband, also a psychiatric social worker, once worked in a mental health clinic that served individuals with chronic schizophrenia. People with schizophrenia often hear voices we cannot hear, see things we don't see, and feel others are out to get them. They also have a poor sense of boundaries (i.e., they don't understand why standing 2 inches from someone's face when talking to them makes them back up, that 5-minute hugs and 3-minute handshakes make people uncomfortable, and that you shouldn't tell people everything about yourself and your family 5 minutes after you meet them). One client, unable to drive, relied on buses for transportation to and from his various destinations. He had the uncanny habit of getting on every bus he rode and announcing, "Hi! I'm Z and I'm a paranoid schizophrenic!" Naturally, people got nervous and moved away from him. This behavior hurt Mr. Z's feelings, but he never understood the connection between his comments and people's reactions. One day my husband, creative social worker that he is, decided to help Mr. Z by role-playing appropriate bus behavior. Mr. Z's group pretended it was going for a bus ride and my husband was the driver. They all stood at make-believe bus stops and greeted the driver and other passengers with a hello or how are you today when they boarded the imaginary bus. When the bus came to Mr. Z's stop he started to make his usual comment and other group members quickly reminded him that saying hello was *all* he needed to say. It took many practice sessions but Mr. Z finally learned not to blurt out news of his mental illness in the presence of strangers. He also learned that at home, with family or with good friends, he *could* talk about his illness without being rejected.

THE ABSENCE OF EFFECTIVE COPING SKILLS

When faced with situations that create pain, fear, or confusion people generally respond in one of three ways: They withdraw and refuse to take any action, they become defensive to keep others from seeing their vulnerabilities, or they activate patterns of behavior that proved helpful in the past. Unfortunately, these response choices often make matters worse. Avoiding issues doesn't make them go away, it simply delays the inevitable. Becoming defensive creates hostility in others at times when you most need their support. Relying on coping skills that worked in the past *may* help, but often, like my hip hugger jeans from the 70's, they just don't fit anymore! Relapse prevention, learning what can be done *instead of* avoiding, acting out, or relying on outdated coping skills, is the key to managing almost any disabling condition. We will discuss this further in chapters 12 and 13 when we explore strategies for living effectively with mental illness.

EXHAUSTION

Have you ever been so tired that you just couldn't go on? I remember when I was in graduate school my days were often 18 to 20 hours long. I would look longingly at *any* flat surface and dream of curling up for a 10-minute nap to refresh myself. Of course I never had 10 minutes for a nap! Luckily for me graduate school was time limited. I knew that for 2 years I would be exhausted and overwhelmed. What got me through that experience was knowing that in 24 months I would get my life back.

Being exhausted takes a toll on one's physical and mental health. It makes us irritable, interferes with our ability to think clearly and logically, and when chronic creates depression and hopelessness. Individuals wearing masks to hide symptoms of their mental illness frequently exist in a state of chronic exhaustion. Unlike my graduate school experience there is no end in sight, no way to identify when the exhaustion will end. Battling the symptoms of their illness under cover, struggling to present a facade of wellness, denying how ill they are for fear of being labeled or ridiculed, they expend huge amounts of energy just surviving. Like a gas guzzling car, they eventually come to a point where the tank is empty. Unfortunately, they cannot go to the local fuel station and replenish their energy when it finally plays out. The exhaustion that springs from trying to be something one is not leads to self-hatred, social isolation, anger toward others, depression, a sense of futility, tunnel vision, and in some cases, suicide. An example will help illustrate how dangerous chronic exhaustion is, especially to those struggling with mental illness.

Too Tired to Care

Ms. AA was a woman in her late 20's who had struggled all her life. A victim of child abuse, life had been one battle after another for as long as she could remember. She was sexually abused by her stepfather from ages 6 to 10 at which time her mother "caught them in the act." Since her mother blamed Ms. AA for this sexual activity she was placed in foster care and never saw her family again. Between the ages of 10 and 15 Ms. AA lived in five foster homes. She was physically abused in two, sexually abused in one, and treated "tolerably in the remaining two." She left home at 15 and lived on the streets, resorting to prostitution to survive. At age 18 Ms. AA was almost beaten to death by her pimp. She escaped to another city to begin anew. She sought the help of a battered women's shelter and put her life together. She went back to school and got a job in a local department store. At 22 Ms. AA married her husband. The marriage initially went well but as time passed, he became verbally and physically abusive. She never knew when he would blow up, and she lived in a constant state of fear. Ms. AA became very depressed and attempted suicide by overdosing on Valium she had gotten from her family doctor to help her sleep better. She continued in this relationship for another 5 years before finally realizing that if she stayed she would die.

When I met Ms. AA she was very depressed and saw herself as a terrible, stupid, worthless person. She could not identify *any* positive things about herself and when I attempted to identify strengths for her, she withdrew even further into her shell. Ms. AA was exhausted. Her entire life had been a struggle for survival and she saw no end in sight. At age 29 she was burned

out, used up, and rapidly approaching a point of hopelessness
that, unless interrupted, would eventually lead to another suicide attempt. Ms. AA spent 30 days in the hospital being treated
for posttraumatic stress disorder (PTSD) and depression. She
was then enrolled in a long-term outpatient women's group.
During her 2 years in this group Ms. AA reviewed the events
in her life and realized that she was not to blame. She gradually
began to identify strengths and recognized her right to happiness and good relationships. Ms. AA went back to school and
got a degree in computer programming. She moved into a
nicer apartment and made several women friends. As time
passed, she began to look less stressed. She gained weight, her
hair regained its shine. She started paying more attention to
her makeup and clothing. She carried herself with pride and
developed self-confidence. When therapy ended Ms. AA had
come to terms with her past and placed it in perspective so it
would not continue to consume her present and future. She
realized that PTSD and depression are chronic mental illnesses
and that she would need periodic treatment during stressful
times in her life. She learned relapse prevention skills to help
her recognize when symptoms were increasing and developed
skills to reverse this process. Although Ms. AA's case ended
successfully, for many others in states of chronic exhaustion,
the result is premature death from suicide. If *you* or someone
you love suffers from chronic exhaustion get help now! It could
mean the difference between life and death.

LEARNED HELPLESSNESS

Learned helplessness is the result of chronic, uninterrupted
exhaustion and defeat. When individuals *believe* there is no
hope for recovery, that they will always be miserable and exhausted, they often reach a point of emotional surrender. They
simply stop trying to get better. They are so beaten down that
even when help is offered they are too tired to accept it or

don't believe it will help so refuse to try. If you have ever been to a nursing home you have probably seen learned helplessness. I was a nurse's aide one summer and got a real taste of how disabling learned helplessness can be.

As people come to believe they have no control in their lives, they surrender all desire to help themselves. Even when they are physically able to feed, dress, and toilet themselves, they act "as if" they cannot. (This is not to be confused with stubbornness or willful behavior. These people genuinely believe they are helpless even when provided with evidence that shows them they are not.) They will go without eating unless someone feeds them, stay in pajamas all day, and sit in urine and feces, even when it blisters their skin, unless someone changes them. They *believe* they are helpless; therefore, they become helpless.

Learned helplessness is a frequent visitor to those afflicted with chronic mental illness. As symptoms become more pronounced, it takes greater effort to keep the mask of normalcy in place. Since those wearing masks cannot ask for help, they struggle to keep up the image of wellness when inside they are dying an inch at a time. Each day becomes a battle to get from morning to night with as little pain as possible. As efforts to keep the mask in place become more difficult, they withdraw hoping others won't notice. Spending day after day with only negative thoughts for company they eventually reach a point of indifference. Life is a painful struggle without pleasure or joy. They see no point in trying since past efforts changed nothing and current efforts are more trouble than they are worth. If someone sees through their mask and encourages them to come out from behind it they often refuse, too tired to take it off and not willing to let someone else remove it for them.

People who reach this point rarely come in for treatment—they are simply too tired to bother. We sometimes see them in emergency rooms or on locked psychiatric wards following suicide attempts, but the potential for change, once it progresses this far, is very small. The lesson to be learned: If you wear a mask, or know someone who does, take it off or encourage them to before it's too late. Like a woman with breast cancer who does not seek treatment until it's too late, people with mental illness can also wait too long. Don't let yourself or someone you love become a statistic!

This chapter provided an overview of five factors that seriously erode our ability to remove the masks that shield us from our own reality. "Buying into" social attitudes that mental illness somehow transforms people into dangerous, second-class citizens prevents those afflicted from reaching for help and the rest of us from offering it. Since negative social attitudes are born of ignorance, and many of us are ignorant about mental illness and the people it affects, we can start learning today! There are no acceptable excuses for refusing to learn about something that affects over 51 million Americans each year! As a society we can slowly change social attitudes so those affected can remove their masks without fear of rejection or abandonment. This will pave the way for removal of two additional barriers: exhaustion and learned helplessness. Finally, we can develop relapse prevention skills to improve our management of symptoms and cope with the symptoms of those we love. The first step in this process is learning how to be real so we can guide others through this process. This will be the focus of the final four chapters in this book.

PART III

ON BECOMING REAL

"What is real?" asked the Rabbit one day, when they were lying side by side near the nursery fender, before Nana came to tidy the room. "Does it mean having things that buzz inside you and a stick-out handle?"

"Real isn't how you are made," said the Skin Horse. "It's a thing that happens to you. When a child loves you for a long, long time, not just to play with, but REALLY loves you, then you become Real."

"Does it hurt?" asked the Rabbit.

"Sometimes," said the Skin Horse because he was always truthful.

"When you are Real you don't mind being hurt."

"Does it happen all at once, like being wound up," he asked, "or bit by bit?"

"It doesn't happen all at once," said the Skin Horse. "You become. It takes a long time. That's why it doesn't often happen to people who break easily, or have sharp edges, or who have to be carefully kept. Generally, by the time you are Real, most of your hair has been loved off, and your eyes drop out and you get loose in the joints and very shabby. But these things don't matter at all, because once you are Real you can't be ugly, except to people who don't understand."

Reprinted with permission from *The Velveteen Rabbit or, How Toys Become Real*, copyright 1991, by Running Press, Philadelphia, PA.

133

CHAPTER 11

DYING TO BE REAL

The story of *The Velveteen Rabbit* is one of my favorite childhood stories. If you have not read it I encourage you to do so at your earliest convenience. This story is about a velveteen rabbit's desire to be more than a plush toy. As the story unfolds he undergoes the process of becoming real. The story has a happy ending—the velveteen rabbit, tattered and frayed from years of loving, is transformed into a real rabbit and dances off into the forest to live happily ever after among his own kind.

The velveteen rabbit paid a price for becoming real. He spent years being kissed, hugged, and dragged around. He was tossed into toy boxes, thrown haphazardly into corners, and stuffed under beds. Subjected to the whims of the little boy who owned him, life was sometimes pleasant and at other times frightening. On several occasions his existence was threatened by the child's nanny who wanted to burn or throw him away because she thought him beyond salvation (i.e., too old and ugly to repair). The little rabbit, with the guidance and encouragement of the skin horse, held onto his desire to be real until it came true. Yes, becoming real was costly to the velveteen rabbit, but the alternative was much more costly. He would have been being burned, tossed out with the trash, or boxed up in the attic until someone found and discarded him years later.

Individuals with mental illnesses are a lot like the velveteen rabbit. They wear masks to hide who they really are from the people who wouldn't understand. Those who are lucky find someone, like the skin horse, who offers encouragement and support during the process of self-discovery. Individuals willing to experience the fear and pain of taking off their masks gradually become real. They come to realize that *all* human beings, themselves included, have beauty and value regardless of what others say. Becoming real means facing the reactions of self and others as the essence of one's being is unveiled. The reward: self-acceptance and freedom to embrace and participate in life with *all* its joys and sorrows. Realizing that the journey, not the destination, is what life is all about.

What happens to individuals who resist becoming real? Life is transformed into a frantic struggle to maintain images created to fool themselves and others. Unfortunately, this desperate masquerade is very self-destructive. Many, believing self-discovery is too painful, resist the urge to become real. The result: a life sentence of isolation and misery. For others life becomes a concrete box: dark, damp, cold, and frightening. Trapped beneath their masks, suicide is the only known means of escape. Tragically, they fail to realize that the box, like their mask, is an illusion—it exists only in their minds. If this fact becomes known before it is too late they discover a chisel and hammer inside their concrete box, which have been there all the time so they can set themselves free. Let's look at what happens when individuals believe removing their mask, becoming real, is more frightening than death.

THE MAN WHO COULD NOT DIE

Mr. BB, a man in his early 50's, has suffered from depression and posttraumatic stress disorder (PTSD) since childhood. He was physically and sexually abused as a child then further traumatized during the Vietnam War. Each time life dealt him a ladle of pain, he became more strongly convinced that death was the only cure for his suffering. Mr. BB has, to date, attempted suicide 10 times. He slit his wrists twice, jumped off a bridge, attempted to asphyxiate himself with exhaust fumes from his car, overdosed on pills and alcohol five times, and shot himself in the head. After his last attempt I visited him in the hospital to help him explore the forces that drive him repeatedly to the brink of suicide. Mr. BB's rationale is simple: Life is a painful reality, death a pathway to peace. He believes that death, although final, means no longer having to face the daily struggle of living. For Mr. BB life has been more painful than rewarding so he doesn't feel he has much to lose by dying. He is, however, willing to consider options since after 10 suicide attempts he thinks there might be a reason he cannot die.

The most challenging part of working with Mr. BB is the depth of his hopelessness. Having experienced a lifetime of pain, he believes that, for him, there are no options. That life has always been and will always be filled with disappointments and pain. His negative attitude freezes him into a position of powerlessness and inaction. The first step in Mr. BB's recovery involved identifying his mask. To become real, he had to identify the image he used to avoid his true self. He presents a sad, defeated figure, describing himself as "a shell of a man." A childhood filled with negative messages convinced him he was stupid and worthless. His self-esteem, seriously damaged during this onslaught, taught him to believe he was unworthy of happiness and peace. Sadly, he never realized that once grown he could challenge and change this negative and self-destructive image. His first mask was the ugly duckling. The little boy who was told he was ugly, awkward, could never fit in, and was unlovable, became a man who *believed* he was ugly, awkward, never fit in, and was unlovable. To defend against the enormous emotional pain created by this mask, he created a second, more deadly mask: the inside-out porcupine. Mr. BB *never* expresses his anger or frustration to others (after all, worthless people have no right to state their feelings and needs). For as far back as he can remember he turned anger inward, blaming himself for the events of his life (many of which were beyond his control). Unable to believe he might have value to someone, he repeatedly attempts suicide to escape the pain of "knowing" he is a burden to himself and others and would be better off dead.

Once Mr. BB identified these masks, he was invited to explore the messages that created and sustained them. He discovered his image of himself, a worthless, stupid, hopeless individual who could never do anything right, came from childhood messages received before, during, and after episodes of physical and sexual abuse. Because this abuse continued for many years he came to believe himself the "cause"; therefore, he *must* be very bad and unlovable for others to treat him so cruelly. He was encouraged to share these thoughts in group so other members could give him feedback about the accuracy of these statements. After months of treatment he got up the courage to share his thoughts. Group members challenged his self-image, providing many examples of strengths he could draw on in times of desperation. Over the next 18 months he slowly and painfully moved closer to becoming real. Mr. BB has a long way to go, but has not attempted suicide in almost a year. He can now identify several options, other than suicide, for managing negative feelings. Mr. BB has come to understand that he *does* have value on the basis of his existence; that no more is needed. He is learning not to waste energy fretting over the "if only's, should's, ought to be's, and can never be's" in his life, and is beginning to work on "what is and what might be." This shift in Mr. BB's thinking allowed a ray of sunshine to enter his concrete box. He is beginning to believe that maybe, just maybe, there *is* an escape from this box other than death and possibly a glimmer of happiness in his future.

TRAPPED IN THE PAGES

My sister once described her life to me by saying, "Jo, I feel like I'm trapped in the pages of a bad book and can't get out." One day I asked: "Linda, have you considered closing the book or writing a new chapter to create an escape?" Her response,

"Things have gone too far, it's too late. I don't think I *can* change the course of my life." She continued to mask symptoms with the "picture of health," and when no longer able to create this image, retreated behind her caveman mask, preparing to die.

My sister attempted suicide three times before she finally "made it." Each time she begged family members to let her die. The agony caused by symptoms of her mental illness was expressed through these suicide attempts, but I never *really* understood the depth of her pain. I knew she was in pain, and hid behind masks in an attempt to cope with the reality that was her life. We talked about them on several occasions and I begged her to take them off before it was too late. Try as I might, I could not convince her that family and friends would love her for who she really was. What I did not understand until years later is that she could not believe others would love her "real self" because she could not love her "real self." Her fear of being real was so great it extracted the ultimate price: her life. Yes, her pain stopped, but so did all opportunities for growth and change. The cost was also great for those who survived. Her death shattered the hopes, dreams, and hearts of her children and left ragged, ugly scars on the hearts of all who loved her. Like most people who commit suicide her desperate acts were not meant to hurt others. She was in such tremendous emotional pain we simply ceased to be a consideration in her plans. What a tragic end for someone who, had she been able to remove her mask, might have discovered a means to happiness and peace.

Linda's death came when I least expected it. She had become more active with family and friends and I thought she was doing better. She truly was an expert at wearing masks and hers was deadly! If like Linda, you wear a mask, take it off before it's too late! The people who really matter will provide love and support in your struggle to become real. If someone you love is hiding behind a mask, take your best shot at helping them remove it, but realize, as I did, that your power is limited.

They *alone* have the power to decide whether to keep hiding, struggle to become real, or die. Linda's belief that her concrete box was impervious kept her from looking for a way out—don't let this happen to you! If you can't find a way out on your own *get help*! There are endless options for change in life but no options, at least not in this world, in death.

THE WALKING WOUNDED

Mr. CC, a man in his late 40's, witnessed a drowning at age 22 that left one man dead and many emotionally traumatized. This incident profoundly changed Mr. CC's self-image since he was unable to prevent the other man's death. His agony over this accident, and his inability to change the outcome, have led him to chronic thoughts of suicide. Life has become a daily struggle. The goal: to get through just one more day "for the family." His wife and children live in constant fear that someday they will come home and find him dead. Mr. CC is trapped in a concrete box constructed of painful memories he cannot forget. Trying to place these memories in perspective (i.e., helping him remember, work through, and let go of—not *forget*—these memories) has been unsuccessful because he feels his punishment for not saving the person who drowned is a lifetime of painful memories and regrets.

His chronic suicidality creates such tension that it threatens to destroy every member of his family. His spouse, trapped by *her* belief that she alone is responsible for saving his life, is frozen in a terror, always watchful lest he kill himself and make her liable. He stays alive to keep from hurting her but hurts her even more with constant threats of suicide. She watches to keep him safe, increasing his risk by playing the game. The children have escaped to college to distance themselves from this destructive drama. Is Mr. CC a bad or willful man? Does he deliberately set out to make his own and others' lives a living hell? *No!* He is an intelligent, sensitive, caring person trapped in a box from which he believes there is no escape save death. His sense of powerlessness keeps him from seeking the key that might free him and may, ultimately, lead to his death.

Why then, if options for change are possible, don't Mr. BB and CC race toward them with open arms? Why did Linda kill herself if options exist that could have saved her life and made it less painful? The answer, in part, is because none of them *believed* that options exist or they were or are just too tired to try anymore. In order to reverse this destructive process three key ingredients must be present: First, individuals must identify the mask they wear, the reasons they wear it, and be willing to work toward removing it. Second, they must learn to identify warning signs of increasing distress and develop and apply a series of coping skills to interrupt this process before it is too late. Finally, they must learn the art of self-acceptance. People, like paintings, are works in progress. The process of self-discovery and personal growth, whether mentally ill or not, continues for as long as we live. Each time we add what we think are the "final touches," something else pops up demanding our attention! The focus of the final three chapters of this book is on becoming real. On acquiring and applying the ingredients identified above that can, and often do, mean the difference between life and death.

CHAPTER 12

AWARENESS: THE FIRST STEP

The first step of changing anything in our lives is recognizing what we need to change. In this case it means identifying the mask(s) we wear and understanding why we wear them. This complicated process requires careful self-examination. Try and remember the first time you noticed yourself wearing a mask. Ask yourself the following questions:

1. *Who* were you with when you put on your mask?
2. *What* were you doing that made wearing a mask necessary?
3. *When* did you realize your mask was "on"?
4. *Where* were you when you put on your mask?
5. *Why* did you feel a need to hide your "real self"?
6. *How* has your pattern of using a mask(s) developed across time?

Your answers to these questions are vital to the process of self-awareness and change. All behavior is called into play by "environmental cues" (what is happening around us and what we *think* about what is happening around us). When we *believe* a situation resembles one from our past, we respond exactly as we did in the previous situation. Over time our patterns of response are automatically activated when we perceive current situations are similar to those we experienced before. An example will help you better understand this process.

THE HUNGRY DOG

As a child I had a wonderful dog named Sugar. Her daily routine included breakfast at 7:00 A.M., a walk when I got home from school, and dinner at 5:00 P.M.. As Sugar aged, she began putting on weight. The veterinarian instructed me to feed her only once daily, in the morning, so she could "burn off" calories throughout the day. I began this new routine and Sugar, accustomed to being fed twice daily, was quite beside herself. The first day of this new schedule she paced, whined, and barked when 5:00 P.M. came and went without the usual appearance of food. When these antics failed she dropped her bowl in front of my feet and gave me a pitiful look. Sugar was "conditioned" to being fed twice each day. She expected these feedings and never thought about them until they didn't happen. She simply showed up at the appointed time twice each day. When the routine changed she did not know how to act so she became distressed. Her automatic response (show up at the feeding dish at 7:00 A.M. and 5:00 P.M. expecting food) no longer "fit" since the feeding at 5:00 P.M no longer existed. Sugar was forced to change her response (show up for food only at 7:00 A.M.) since showing up at 5:00 P.M. no longer produced a reward. Awareness that 5:00 P.M. no longer meant food was the first step in Sugar's behavior change (no longer going to the food dish at 5:00 P.M.).

Human beings are no different from dogs when it comes to conditioned responses. We, too, "learn" to respond in certain ways depending on the situation at hand. Identifying risk factors that shape our behavior helps us understand why we act as we do. Therefore, removing the mask(s) that hide symptoms of mental illness requires us to recognize the *reasons* we put masks on (see chapters 1 and 10 for a review of reasons why people wear masks). Once this is accomplished, we must develop strategies for approaching situations where we formerly wore masks with responses that allow us to be real. This chapter identifies risk factors that send people running for their masks.

The following chapter introduces strategies to remove these deadly masks and replace them with healthier responses.

How does one recognize that the risk of putting one's mask on is increasing? Substance abusers at risk of returning to drinking or drug use rely on a process known as *relapse prevention.* This process allows individuals to identify risk factors that increase their relapse potential and interrupt this process before it is too late. When applied to the use of masks to hide psychiatric symptoms, relapse prevention means recognizing factors that lead individuals to raise a mask instead of showing their real selves to the world. Relapse prevention makes good sense for substance abusers who risk illness and death unless they stop drinking and using drugs. It makes equally good sense for mentally ill people at risk of experiencing an increase in symptoms and/or death unless they learn to remove their masks. Let's take a closer look at what relapse prevention really means and how it can be used to remove the deadly masks identified in chapters 3 to 8 of this book.

The word *relapse* means returning to previous patterns of behavior. This involves a *gradual* change in thinking, feeling, and acting that ultimately results in activation of our old behaviors. For example, if I am a "recovering chocoholic" my goal is to never eat chocolate again. As I enter the relapse process I begin *thinking* about how much I love chocolate, about how I *should* be able to eat it. This leads me to *feel* angry and deprived. I may begin *stopping by the donut shop* to smell the chocolate donuts. The longer this process continues, the more likely it becomes that one day when I walk into the donut shop I will order and eat a dozen chocolate donuts!

For individuals with mental illnesses relapse involves an increase in symptoms accompanied by attempts to hide these symptoms behind a mask. The more severe the symptoms, the more energy is needed to hide them from the outside world. As this process continues, the individual experiences a change in how they *feel* (they may become more depressed or anxious, depending on what illness they have). This brings about changes in *thinking* (they may begin to have thoughts about stopping their prescribed medication, running away, or suicide). Then *behavior* begins to change (they become withdrawn or hostile). This stressful process, unless interrupted, finally results in decompensation (they get sicker) or death (suicide).

Relapse, as demonstrated above, is a *process* not a discrete event. This means it happens gradually. Unfortunately, changes in feelings, thinking, and behaving are so subtle that individuals in relapse are unaware until they suddenly find themselves in great distress. Relapse is analogous to the process of growing old. You don't "suddenly" wake up old, it's a gradual process that happens over a period of years. Most people begin to get wrinkles and gray hair in their 40's. This gradual decline in appearance and body functions continues until we die. Like the relapse process, aging has many "warning signs." Those who make adjustments along the way generally have an easier transition into old age. Those who attempt to deny it have an emotional crisis when they finally realize they are old. It makes sense to prepare ourselves along the way, both to identify and cope with warning signs of relapse *and* old age, doesn't it?

If relapse is the return to former patterns of behavior what, then, is relapse prevention? Relapse prevention is a *process* that involves recognizing the triggers that increase our risk of reactivating former patterns of behavior and developing specific skills to interrupt this process. Gorski and Miller (1986; see the Suggested Reading List under "Relapse Prevention") provide an excellent book and workbook for substance abusers which attempts to identify and interrupt the relapse process. The present book focuses on relapse prevention as it applies to mental illness, identifying triggers that generate the masks used to hide symptoms of mental illness.

Relapse triggers can be but are not always person or illness specific. This means relapse triggers may or may not be shared by other people, even if their diagnosis is the same as yours. For example, a combat veteran with posttraumatic stress disorder

(PTSD) might consider July 4th a relapse trigger because fire-works often trigger memories of war. A rape victim with PTSD might identify certain sights (people who look like their at-tacker) as relapse triggers. A person with a fear of snakes might identify a trip to the snake house at the zoo as a relapse trigger, whereas a person with a fear of heights would find a trip to the top of the Empire State Building a relapse trigger. When identifying relapse triggers it is *very important* to list triggers that apply to *you*. The following list of risk factors serves only as a starting point and is by no means complete. Use it as a guide adding and removing risk factors as necessary. Make a written list of the triggers you identify as factors in your relapse process so you can refer to it when we begin looking at interven-tion tools in chapter 13. Let's look at the risk factors I have identified during my 10 years in psychiatry that are noteworthy in individuals with mental illnesses. As you review this list, real-ize you can have *many* risk factors and that each risk factor may intensify the negative effects of others. This will become especially important when we begin to develop relapse preven-tion tools in chapter 13.

RISK FACTORS

NEGATIVE THOUGHTS

This risk factor, fed by stigmatizing social attitudes, coupled with a healthy dose of low self-esteem, leads individuals to as-sume a negative view of themselves and their potential for a fulfilling life. They tend to adopt a "my cup is half empty" attitude about life and are skeptical that things can ever change. This in turn increases symptoms of their psychiatric condition and encourages the use of porcupine and warrior masks. After all, if I present an angry and unreachable front nobody will try and get close to me. This gives me more ammu-nition to make the world a terrible place (see, I *told you* nobody cares)! Negative thinking is like pus in a wound. If you don't remove it, the wound festers and grows more infected which creates an ever widening circle of damage. If it goes too far, individuals find themselves in concrete boxes with the belief that no tools, save death, can release them.

NEGATIVE FEELINGS

Negative feelings rob individuals of all hope, leaving them empty and numb. Like yeast in bread dough, they rise slowly, often undetected until they are so powerful they immobilize the bearer. Negative feelings, when combined with negative thoughts, create learned helplessness. Affected individuals come to believe that no matter what they do life can and will never change. They resign themselves to lives filled with misery or premature death. Peace of mind shattered, dreams destroyed, energy drained, hope snuffed out, no reason to keep on living. They slide toward an abyss of self-destruction and often, even when a life-saving rope is thrown within their reach, are too tired to reach out and grab it.

TUNNEL VISION

Tunnel vision is like blinders on a racehorse. You can only see what is *directly* in front of you! This severely limits our ability to identify and apply options that might change the current situation. Individuals with tunnel vision gradually lose their ability to see options. This process is so subtle they often resist and deny that change is possible even when confronted with firm evidence that options for change exist. Tunnel vision is a by-product of negative thoughts and feelings and becomes a frame of reference for all life experiences. Those affected become color blind, losing the ability to see the hundreds of colors that exist on the color wheel of life. Sadly, this narrow world view dooms them to stagnation, and in some cases, death.

NEGATIVE SELF-ESTEEM

Self-esteem is our *personal* view of our value to self and others. We begin developing this "self-opinion" in infancy and it is shaped by the experiences of our lives. When experiences are positive and we are nurtured by others who praise and love us, self-esteem is positive. However, when experiences are negative, and we are abused or neglected by others, self-esteem becomes negative. Individuals with mental illnesses are especially "at risk" for negative self-esteem by virtue of their differences. Living in a society that prizes individuality, upward mobility, and conformity makes it very difficult for members who are unable, because of their disability, to aspire to these lofty American ideals.

Comparing ourselves to others is foolish because there are always those who are either more or less successful than we are. Despite this reality, from an early age we are "taught" to compare ourselves to others, to outdo our peers. This drive for achievement causes many of us to lose ourselves along the way. It is especially painful for our mentally ill members who, like shetland ponies in a race with thoroughbreds, lack the ability to compete effectively. In a society with narrow and rigid definitions of happiness and success they are doomed to failure before they even begin. Self-definition, based on existing social attitudes and values, reinforces their belief that as "second class citizens" they would not really be missed if they simply ceased to be.

PEER PRESSURE TO CONFORM

Peer pressure is another risk factor created by current social attitudes and values. This is especially true for individuals with mental illnesses since they "look" and "seem" so normal. When disabilities are invisible society tends to frown on those who claim illness, even when they present evidence to support their claim. Those unable to work, to establish and maintain relationships, to function "normally" in society, are scorned and ridiculed. They are constantly challenged to "try harder," "be responsible," "stop goofing off." This constant pressure to "be normal" drives many to continuous attempts to become "normal" with disastrous results. Repeated failure, especially when one is giving it one's best shot, destroys self-esteem, creates negative thoughts and feelings, and encourages individuals to wear masks lest they be detected and singled out. They "learn" how to make "politically correct" responses to questions like, "What do you do for a living?" "Where do you work?" "Can you believe those clowns on disability who claim to be mentally ill, they look healthier than I am!" Yes, peer pressure creates tremendous stress for those with mental illnesses who are literally dying to be real.

Unrealistic Expectations

Close on the heels of peer pressure comes unrealistic expectations. After all, if society, if my own family thinks I can be normal, then raise the anchor and full steam ahead! The desire to "be normal," to achieve what others can, creates the dangerous "picture of health" mask (see chapter 3). Determined to fit in if it kills them, many do indeed die trying. When someone is missing a leg, suffers from mental retardation, has an eye missing, we make exceptions, adjust our expectations so they can achieve their highest level of functioning given their disabling condition. This is not true for mentally ill individuals who "look so normal." We expect, no demand, that they "get with the program" and pull their weight. Constant peer pressure breeds unrealistic expectations leading them to try, fail, try again, fail again. Years of repeated failure fuel negative thoughts, feelings, self-esteem, and a sense of futility about life. If I try my best and cannot succeed, if others laugh at or ridicule me rather than offering compassion and support, what's the use!? Life is so hard and being unable to carry what is identified as one's fair share of the load often leads to burnout, decompensation (getting sicker), and death.

SOCIAL ISOLATION

When subjected to prolonged periods of isolation humans perish from loneliness and self-neglect. The caveman mask (see chapter 4) and the ugly duckling mask (see chapter 8) thrive on isolation and are deadly. Social isolation fuels negative thoughts and feelings, reinforces negative self-esteem, and leaves individuals feeling abandoned, misunderstood, and forgotten. Avoiding others in order to prevent detection, they unknowingly create a trap that moves them ever closer to self-destruction. Desperate attempts to project an image of self-sufficiency lead to fear, hopelessness, and apathy. The longer one stays in seclusion, the harder it is to reach out, even when others reach first. A vicious cycle of isolation, feeling bad because one is isolated, withdrawing further to cope with the negative feelings about being isolated, feeds feelings that one is worthless. When isolated there is no one to challenge these negative thoughts and feelings so they continue to grow until the emotional pain becomes so intense we seek help or die.

DESIRE TO TEST THE LIMITS/DENIAL

This risk factor, fueled by unrealistic expectations and the desire to conform, leads individuals to challenge their need for ongoing care. After all, since I *look* so normal and *feel* so good, why should I keep taking medication, attend therapy sessions, monitor my feelings, thoughts, and behavior? Individuals with mental illnesses frequently "test the limits" with negative results: Symptoms get worse, they begin to act out in public, or withdraw into self-imposed seclusion. The desire to "be normal" is often so great they sacrifice the mental health they still possess trying to achieve the impossible.

A person with a heart condition wouldn't ignore chest pains, so why do individuals with mental illnesses ignore warning signs that symptoms are increasing? Again, society validates the patient with chest pains but scrutinizes the one who reports symptoms of mental illness. *Testing limits is a form of denial.* Maybe if I don't look at it, it won't be true. Tragically, like a man with lung cancer who dies a painful death because he refused to seek medical care early, mentally ill individuals often become so sick before they seek help that it dramatically interferes with their recovery.

SHAME

A great catalyst for the ugly duckling mask (see chapter 8), shame generates all nature of negative thoughts and feelings. Individuals with mental illnesses often feel ashamed to acknowledge their condition to others. After all, who wants to admit they have a mental problem, right? Current social attitudes make it difficult for mentally ill individuals *not* to feel shame. The stigma of being honest about one's mental illness interferes with employment (after all, if you put "Yes" on an application that asks if you have ever had psychiatric care you can forget *that* job, despite the Americans with Disabilities Act). Mental illness reduces one's potential for establishing a relationship (who wants to date a mental patient?). Mental illness "marks" individuals as "unstable, unpredictable, high risk for problems" (greatly reducing their ability to participate fully in society). Well, anything that limits life so dramatically would naturally create shame in those affected. The belief that they "caused it" (e.g., combat veterans who feel PTSD is their penance for acts of war), that they don't "deserve better" (an individual with schizophrenia whose family abandoned him), that if they only "tried harder" they could get it together (the depressed patient who simply cannot get up enough energy to return to the classroom).

Shame is a great disabler and creates more emotional pain than any psychiatric illness ever could. Since mental illnesses are identified as diseases, not simply illusions of the mind, why does shame continue? Again, social attitudes and ignorance about what mental illness really is and isn't. Social attitudes plus negative self-image equals shame. Shame generates a desire to mask symptoms which interferes with individuals' willingness to seek treatment. Shame damages lives, shame distorts reality, shame kills.

SELF-PITY

Self-pity is the wrecking ball of self-esteem and destroyer of present and future happiness. Rising from the "if only's" of life, self-pity breeds contempt, jealousy, bitterness, and anger. Self-pity is the act of reviewing all the short-comings of one's life and focusing on how much one has lost without considering what one has gained. It is a constant focus on the negative, the bad, the unfortunate, the unfair, and the unjust. Individuals with mental illnesses are at risk of falling into the self-pity trap because they are intelligent people who know all too well what they have lost and what can never be regained. They become bitter because those around them thrive and prosper while they suffer and stagnate. Doomed to carry extra lead in their saddle-bags, they waste energy resenting those whose load is lighter rather than attempting to redistribute the load.

Bitterness breeds self-contempt leading to self-destructive thoughts, feelings, and behavior. Why care when nothing can change the fact that a disability is part of my life? Why try when I can never reach the dream I lived my life for. Why draw up new blueprints for life when there is no guarantee that fate won't once again snatch it from me? Self-pity in small doses is harmless and cleansing. Self-pity on a regular basis is dangerous and exhausting. It robs us of our potential to grieve losses, build new dreams, and embrace life to the fullest. Life becomes nothing more than the bitter reality of what we have lost with no hope that things will ever get better. With this risk factor in full swing, why even keep on living? After all, it can only get worse—can't it?

IMPATIENCE

America, the land of deadlines, quotas, numbers, statistics, units of production, and cut-off points. Is it any wonder we want it all and yesterday would be just fine thank you? Patience may be a virtue but not one many Americans have (myself included)! In a society as upwardly mobile and achievement oriented as ours, is it any wonder those with disabilities become impatient when they participate in treatment and don't get immediate and miraculous results? When you have experienced years of emotional pain, social isolation, feeling you are insignificant, wouldn't you be eager to reverse this trend? When you put every ounce of your being into changing current life circumstances, wouldn't you expect things to get much better, and fast?

Such is the basis for disenchantment and disgust! Although a great ideal, the reality is that anything worthwhile generally involves time, effort, and sacrifice. Even when we put forth our best efforts, we don't always get what we want or have things turn out as planned. Because mental illness is treatable, not curable, people get disgusted with treatment. They want a "feel good" experience and what therapy initially produces is an *increase* in pain and discomfort as they wade through years of emotional waste. I always warn my clients that it gets worse before it gets better, it hurts more before it feels good, that the only way out is through, and there are no guarantees except that if you *don't* do something, it will definitely get worse. Sounds rather pessimistic you say? Well, I'm a firm believer in setting out the realities before we begin so there are no surprises later! In general these comments help people cope with their impatience by validating how hard recovery is.

Impatience is a risk factor because it makes people give up too soon, expect the unrealistic, and feel dissatisfied if they get less than they planned for. In our "instant" society, we find waiting 4 minutes for a baked potato to cook in the microwave intolerable, so how can we blame mentally ill individuals for becoming angry when, in spite of their best efforts, they just can't get up the hill? Maybe we should offer them a rope and help pull them up instead of imposing our expectations across the board cookie-cutter style! Maybe we should all offer a little more time and attitude to those who don't quite "fit the mold." Life might run a little less efficiently but it sure would be more worthwhile. Think about it the next time you're steaming because somebody else didn't get something done as quickly and as efficiently as *you* could have done. There just might be a very good reason. Maybe they're marching to a different drummer and doing the best that they can.

SELF-MEDICATING

This refers to the use of drugs or alcohol *or* the abuse of prescription medication in an attempt to contain symptoms. Common rationalizations include: "One pill is good, so why not take two for an even better effect?"; "I only smoke marijuana so I can sleep at night. You'd do it too if you had *my* nightmares"; "What's wrong with a little alcohol? It settles my nerves and makes me feel better." These excuses, although presented very sincerely, can be dangerous. The tendency to self-medicate puts people in a position of "playing doctor." Unless you *are* a doctor, you should never adjust medications without supervision—it can be dangerous. Second, abusing drugs and alcohol only masks symptoms, it doesn't cure them. This allows the disease process to continue so when you *do* finally seek help you will most likely be much sicker than if you had sought it sooner. Self-medication is an early warning sign that you are feeling worse; if you weren't, you would have no need to self-medicate! Use this early warning sign as an opportunity to seek intervention before symptoms become unmanageable.

LOSS OF DAILY STRUCTURE

This risk factor is also a side effect of living in an achievement oriented society. The "empty nest years" and retirement can be difficult for many people because they have depended on their families and careers to structure their time! First the children grow up and leave. You have some struggles but at least you still have work to occupy your time. Twenty years pass and now it's retirement time. Suddenly, there is no need to get up in the morning and race around getting ready for work. There's plenty of time for those things around the house you put off because you've been too busy. You hardly see anyone anymore because all your friends were at your place of employment. Now you are alone, or faced with getting reacquainted with a partner who for years you saw only at night and on weekends and now will be spending 24 hours a day, 7 days a week with. What an adjustment! Well, at least retirement is predictable, something we can plan, right?

What about individuals with mental illnesses that develop during the prime of their lives? Most mental illnesses are diagnosed between one's 18th and 30th birthdays. This is the time in life where work and family are at their zenith. What if you suddenly find yourself too sick to work, stressed out when you have to interact with family members, at a loss of what to do as each minute of the day stretches into hours of dead time? Losing one's daily structure, even at predictable times, like when children leave home and when we retire, requires careful planning so a new structure can be created to provide meaning and purpose in our lives. Those whose daily structure occurs suddenly and "off-time" due to mental illness, not only face the need to restructure their time but the need to grieve what they have lost. All the hopes, dreams, and promises are gone with no idea of what the next step should be. There is no time to plan as there is when one's children begin hitting their teens, as one approaches one's mid-60's and knows retirement looms on the horizon. Loss of structure has a devastating impact on self-esteem which, in situations where individuals already feel "less than" because they are disabled, can be deadly.

OTHER FOCUSED

I cannot count the number of times my clients have said, "Jo, I can't be so selfish as to put my needs first—what would happen to my family?" I often respond by saying, "If you only have three buckets of water left in your well and give it all away, not only will you perish but you will have nothing to give to others in the future. By taking care of your own needs first, you will have energy and resources to help care for others over the long haul." This is contrary to the American values of generosity and self-sacrifice. People carry these values to extremes and sacrifice far more than is healthy or necessary, often with devastating results.

In the case of mental illness, individuals avoid sharing painful feelings because they are afraid of hurting or upsetting other family members. Do you think they would be *less* upset if you get so overwhelmed you kill yourself? Or they don't seek treatment because it costs too much or they can't take off from work—do you think if you put off getting help your symptoms will magically disappear? They will most likely get worse and in the long run will cost more money, more time off work, or disable you completely. This will stress your family much more than the inconvenience caused by seeking help early on!

Self-sacrifice is a virtue unless carried too far, and then it becomes martyrdom! For example, if I am a poor mother and my children are hungry I will certainly do my best to make sure they get as much to eat as possible. If, however, I give them *all* of my food, I will become sick or die and *then* what will become of them? The art of balancing one's focus between individual needs and the needs of one's family is difficult, but remember if you take care of yourself it strengthens the family by reducing the stress they will endure if you don't care for yourself!

SUCCESS AND HAPPY FEELINGS

I can hear you now, "Jo, are you nuts? How can feeling good and having things go well be a trigger?" Well, sometimes when things go too smoothly we forget to remember why it is they are going smoothly (we are following treatment recommendations, keeping our treatment team advised of any changes in mood, behavior, etc.). Success and happy feelings can create an illusion that leads us to "pretend" we're all better. I'm not saying you shouldn't enjoy happy times or that you should panic and expect the worst when things go well. What I am saying is that maintenance of a chronic psychiatric condition, like maintenance on a car, is something that should be done on a regular basis. If things are going well, enjoy, but don't stop taking your medication without a doctor's supervision; don't stop attending recovery meetings; don't stop monitoring your feelings, thoughts, and behavior for the subtle changes that serve as warning signs that symptoms are increasing. Early detection is the key to successful management of a chronic psychiatric illness and takes much less time than waiting until symptoms become unmanageable. Think of it as a daily task, like brushing your teeth. It only takes a few minutes to check out thoughts, feelings, and behavior. A few more to check in with treatment staff or take prescribed medication. By doing maintenance, even when you feel great, it hedges bets in your favor for even more success and happy feelings!

HOLIDAYS, SPECIAL OCCASIONS, ANNIVERSARY DATES

Again, I can hear you saying, "Jo, how can these things be risk factors?" Holidays, special occasions, and anniversary dates are generally more stressful than normal daily life. We interact with more people, are surrounded with more noise and activity, and are called upon to participate in more functions. Even people with no psychiatric conditions agree holidays, anniversaries, and special occasions, although fun, are stressful. For individuals with psychiatric illnesses this added stress can activate symptoms that have been fairly stable. They can trigger memories of the traumatic events that occurred on a particular day, or during a certain month, or around a specific holiday. Sights, sounds, and smells that accompany these risk factors may trigger memories of painful events, increasing anxiety or depression in some individuals.

Does this mean individuals with mental illnesses should avoid holidays, anniversaries, and special occasions? Of course not! The way to safely navigate these factors is to identify specific factors that set off symptoms so you can take action to counteract them. For example, if being in large crowds becomes overwhelming, plan to leave when you begin feeling uncomfortable instead of staying to the bitter end. If July 4th makes you anxious because fire crackers bring back memories of the war, plan a holiday with people in a setting where no fireworks are allowed. If you get depressed seeing families together at Christmas and you have no family, develop a family of friends so during the holidays you won't be alone.

RELATIONSHIP CONFLICTS

An increase in the number of arguments with family members, coworkers, friends, and even strangers, is a warning sign that symptoms are increasing. Irritability is a symptom that one's tolerance for daily stress is shifting. A closer look may help you identify *why* you are so irritable. Often when individuals with mental illnesses begin arguing more frequently it is because they sense (either consciously or unconsciously) the loss of control taking place in their bodies. Irritability, confusion, and decreased tolerance for frustration are early warning signs for many psychiatric disorders. Individuals with depression often experience an irritable mood before major episodes of depression. This is also true for people with bipolar disorders (manic-depression) who frequently become irritable before a manic or depressive episode. Individuals with schizophrenia may become more irritable as their thoughts become less orderly or they experience auditory hallucinations (hear voices) that make them feel threatened. If you notice yourself being "on edge," get feedback from people you trust. If they confirm your suspicion, seek treatment immediately to interrupt this process before it activates the primary symptoms of your particular mental illness.

CHANGES IN SLEEP, DIET, OR EXERCISE PATTERNS

This is a set of risk factors that is frequently overlooked because they are too obvious. I mean, come on, how many people really keep track of how much time they sleep, how their appetite is, whether they are keeping up with their daily exercise plan? Life is too full to analyze such a central part of daily life, isn't it? Yet these are very important risk factors that provide warning signs that symptoms are increasing. If you are a person who generally sleeps 6 to 8 hours nightly and suddenly you begin sleeping only 3 to 4 hours or wake up off and on all night, your body may be trying to tell you something. If you eat a pretty healthy diet and you notice your appetite has decreased and you are losing weight, or you are hungry all the time and eating everything in sight, it may mean something is out of alignment. If you have a consistent exercise plan and just can't seem to get motivated for days at a time, it may be a signal of changes ahead. Our bodies are wonderful machines that give us many, many warning signs when maintenance is needed. No, we don't have all those cool lights on our dashboard like a fancy car, but we *do* have diet, sleep, and exercise habits that change if things aren't quite right. Pay attention to them—it might save you, and your family, a lot of unnecessary stress!

NOT FOR PATIENTS ONLY!

The warning signs listed above are not for patients only. Family members also experience many changes when living with someone who has a chronic psychiatric illness. It is as important to monitor *your* warning signs as it is for the patient to monitor his or hers to prevent burnout, health problems, and mental health problems. Many, many family members end up in doctor's offices asking for medication to combat depression, chronic fatigue, irritability, rashes, infections, headaches, stomachaches, and so forth. These symptoms, frequently the result of prolonged stress, if identified early, are often preventable. Recovery, as you will see in the next chapter, is a family affair.

In closing this chapter, let me repeat how important it is to identify early warning signs of increasing symptoms. The more skilled you become in recognizing when your symptoms are increasing, the better your chances to interrupt the relapse process. Please take a few minutes and think about the risk factors presented above. Write down the ones you have experienced and add others that may not be listed. I encourage you to begin a journal so you can keep track of how these symptoms come into play (the who, what, when, where, why, how) questions I asked early in the chapter. As you begin to understand your buildup process, you will become more skilled in symptom management. One of my clients once said, "How do I know what weapons to use when I don't know what it is I am fighting?" This is precisely *why* learning to recognize your personal risk factors, and the things that set them in motion, is so vital. In order to effectively use the tools identified in the next chapter, you must first accomplish this task. Take it seriously, it could save your life or the life of someone you love.

CHAPTER 13

TOOLS FOR YOUR TOOLBOX

The term *recovery* is frequently misinterpreted to mean "cured." Individuals and family members affected by mental illnesses often believe that a brief hospital stay, medication, and participation in individual or group therapy will result in a return to preillness levels of functioning (i.e., they will be their old selves again after treatment). Another common mistake is for people to compare mental illness with injuries that can be treated and cured: I break my leg, it gets put in a cast to heal, after 6 to 8 weeks the leg is as good as new. I get appendicitis, have an operation to remove my appendix, and I am cured. When this approach is applied to mental illness the interpretation is I felt and acted "crazy," got treatment to help myself feel better, am back to acting and feeling "normal" now, therefore, must be cured.

Mental illness is generally "invisible" unless the individual is experiencing acute symptoms (symptoms severe enough for other people to notice). This lack of "visible" distress or injury often leads the affected individual, family members, and people in general to discount the seriousness of mental disorders (i.e., "I feel fine now so I must be okay"; "You look fine to me, so it can't be that bad"). To help you better understand the chronic nature of mental illness, and how vital ongoing treatment is, let's compare it to an "invisible" medical illness.

163

If an individual has high blood pressure they "look" perfectly normal. They may complain of headaches and feeling tired but little else is noticeable *unless* their blood pressure gets so high they suffer a stroke or heart attack. Once high blood pressure is diagnosed the individual is asked to eliminate salt, alcoholic beverages, cigarettes, and other things that tend to raise blood pressure. Developing a daily exercise routine and practicing stress management to reduce tension are also frequently recommended. If the individual's blood pressure fails to respond to these changes in personal habits medication is added to bring blood pressure into the "normal" range. The individual is not "cured" because if they fall back into old patterns of behavior (stop watching their diet, stop exercising, let stress get the best of them, smoke and drink) blood pressure will once again rise to unsafe levels increasing their risk of heart attack and stroke. While in treatment the disease is in remission (still present in their bodies but symptoms are not active), the individual is controlling symptoms of a chronic disease (high blood pressure). These symptoms can and will become active again if treatment is discontinued.

Mental illness, like high blood pressure, is a chronic condition. Most mental illnesses improve with treatment but are not "cured." When individuals see a psychiatrist regularly, take medications as prescribed, and participate in other recommended activities (treatment varies depending on what illness they have) symptoms become inactive. They are *controlling the symptoms of a chronic disease* (a mental illness). As with high blood pressure the disease is in remission but symptoms can and will become active again if treatment is discontinued. The good news is that although we cannot cure high blood pressure or mental illness both are *treatable.* Symptom management, improved coping skills, and better family communication significantly increase the quality of individual and family life.

So how does one begin this process of removing masks and coping with the symptoms produced by mental illness? The first task, discussed at length in chapter 12, involves identifying risk factors that promote the use of masks to "hide" these symptoms. Removing masks is critical to recovery because masks prevent individuals from seeking early intervention. Postponing treatment allows symptoms to worsen, significantly delaying the recovery process (i.e., with early intervention symptoms might be controlled by adjusting medications in the doctor's office versus delayed intervention which often requires a lengthy hospital stay). Once risk factors are identified individuals must create strategies to manage symptoms *without* their mask! The remainder of this chapter will identify tools, antidotes if you will, to reduce or eliminate these risk factors. I have selected 16 "tools" you may want to add to your recovery toolbox so, without further adieu, let's begin.

Sixteen Tools for Your Toolbox

1. Identifying Personal Risk Factors

Identifying personal risk factors is the first step in creating a recovery toolbox. Please take a few minutes before you read further and review the list of risk factors presented in chapter 12. Take a sheet of paper and write down the ones that cause problems in your life. Identifying *personal* risk factors is important because you cannot reduce their negative effects until you know which ones are affecting you. Once you understand what you're up against, in this case personal risk factors that prevent you from removing your mask, you can acquire proper tools for your toolbox. After identifying personal risk factors, review the list of recovery tools provided below and select those most appropriate at this time in your life.

2. Monitoring for Change

When I ask my clients to monitor their risk factors they usually respond by saying, "Jo! Once we identify risk factors why do we have to *monitor* them? We already know what they are so what's the point?'' My reply: "Changes in how risk factors show up in your life (i.e., you notice an increase in negative thinking, a tendency to isolate more often, feel more depressed than last week, are focused on how awful life is, have an increase in arguments with family members and friends, etc.) are *early warning signs* that symptoms of your illness are increasing. Monitoring increases your ability to detect subtle changes in their presentation. Pay *special attention* to changes in risk factors during times of prolonged stress, anniversary dates, and when things seem to be going a little too smoothly. This will help keep you one step ahead of your symptoms. Early recognition and intervention also reduces the temptation to put on your mask which, as you know, defers but does not prevent disaster!

3. ALLOW OTHERS TO PROVIDE OBJECTIVE FEEDBACK

When it comes to monitoring risk factors, if your nose is too close to the glass, you can't see your face! Sometimes we get so caught up in ourselves we lose sight of the obvious. Allowing close friends, family members, and professionals who work with and know you to provide feedback can identify subtle changes long before they get *your* attention. Since early detection and intervention is the key to successful recovery, allow others to play a role in this process. When someone expresses concern about a particular risk factor, for example says they feel you are more irritable than normal, ask for *specific* feedback. *What* changes have they noticed to raise their concern (what is different about how you look, talk, or act)? *When* did they first notice this change and is it getting worse? Do they have any ideas about *what* factors might be contributing to this change? When in doubt, get feedback from more than one person. If others also report changes in your behavior see your doctor as soon as possible to reduce the risk of relapse.

4. Develop a Support Network

This does *not* mean you have to become socialite of the year!
A support network can be very simple: one or more people
who *really listen* to what you say and feel without judging, blaming, or giving unsolicited advice. Your support network should
be "safe," meaning you feel comfortable enough with those
involved to take off your mask even on really bad days. When
building supports I encourage you to have several resources so
if one is unavailable you have other options (the old don't put
all your eggs in one basket cliché). My clients always laugh
when I say, "Have at least two good friends so if one dies, you
have one left." I am *very* serious about this statement and having lost good friends through death, know what I'm talking
about!

A second, equally important step in building a support network is being willing to use it when you need it. You can have
the most elaborate support network known to man but if you
resist calling it into action when you most need it, it will be
worthless. Many of my clients have crises and refuse to call
others for help, even family members, for fear of upsetting or
angering them. Even those who are *willing supports* are only as
helpful as you allow them to be (this includes your professional
helpers too). Support networks, when built wisely and used
often, enhance self-esteem, provide emotional nourishment
during difficult times, give hope when things appear hopeless,
and reduce the devastating effects of social isolation (depression, feelings of worthlessness and futility, suicidal thinking,
negative thoughts and feelings, shame, etc.).

As I write these "inspiring words" I know you are thinking,
"Yeah Jo, this might be easy for you, but how, with all my
problems, can I possibly build a support network? I who don't
know how to be with people or get anxious in crowds. I who
feel lower than a slug under a rock?" I never *said* it would be
easy but it *can* be done. Just like anything else in life, you start
by taking one step, then another, then another. It will be hard

and scary at first but before you know it you will have at least one or two friends who love and accept you for who you are, tattered edges and all. It's kind of like climbing a ladder. You start at the bottom rung and your destination seems so far away. Each rung you climb brings you closer to the top and, before you know it, you are there! Give it a try, what have you got to lose?

5. WHEN IN DOUBT, CALL IN THE EXPERTS!

Have you ever tried to fix something and because you had *no idea* what you were doing, created a bigger mess than you started with? Boy I have! Once I confused my computer so badly it took a computer expert 2 hours to undo my mistakes. When he finished he said, "Jo, next time, *call me!* If you hadn't kept pushing buttons I could have corrected the problem in a few minutes instead of a few hours. Stick to psychiatry and let *me* take care of the computer!" We all have special talents and mine, obviously, is *not* computers! Psychiatrists, psychologists, and psychiatric social workers are among the "experts in mental health" you can ask to help troubleshoot problems when they arise. Don't tinker around with things you don't understand—see an expert. We don't have all the answers but we can help decrease your symptoms to a manageable level.

6. AVOID ILLICIT DRUGS, ALCOHOL, AND PRESCRIPTION DRUG ABUSE

Many people with mental illnesses use illicit drugs and/or alcohol in an attempt to "self-medicate" symptoms. My strongest recommendation is *don't!* Altering your body chemistry can increase symptoms and may create more problems than it cures. Drugs and alcohol, at best, allow you to temporarily escape from the reality of your situation. They offer no hope of cure and only short-term relief from the symptoms of mental illness or from life problems in general. Abusing prescription medication (not following the directions *exactly* as written) is equally dangerous. (Remember what happened to me when i tinkered with my computer—this could be even worse since we're talking people not machines!) If you have an increase in symptoms, or have difficulty coping with life *call your doctor*—don't play doctor with your own life! Medication, when prescribed by a qualified professional, can help control symptoms making other treatment interventions more effective. Medication, illicit drugs, and alcohol, when misused by individuals with no medical training, make symptoms *worse* and slow the recovery process. Be a smart mental health consumer—*call your doctor!*

7. ADD STRUCTURE TO YOUR LIFE

Many people with mental illnesses are unable to work so spend their time sitting around or watching television. "The life of Riley" we all long for becomes their nightmare: meaningless, with no sense of accomplishment or pleasure. Getting up, when there is nothing to get up for, leads to negative thoughts and feelings, self-pity, poor self-esteem, apathy, helplessness and hopelessness, and social isolation. These ingredients create a powerful casserole called relapse! Even very ill people can learn to structure daily activities so their life has a sense of meaning and purpose. Spend some time talking to vocational counselors, employment specialists, coordinators of volunteer services, and others who might give you ideas of how you can better use your time. Once you create a structure, stick to it!

All human beings need at least a little structure so we know what to do with ourselves. Even the laziest among us become depressed if we never have anything to look forward to. No goals or tasks to accomplish, no product to complete. Lack of structure is a primary risk factor for my clients. It repeatedly aggravates their symptoms making them much sicker than they need to be. Like developing support networks, creating structure in daily life takes time and effort. You must also face and tame your fear of the unknown. I promise once you take that first step it gets easier. There are many wonderful people in life who will encourage and guide you through this process. The first step is planning your plan. Don't delay! The longer you wait the more you'll think about the calamities that might happen if you venture beyond the "uncomfortably familiar" into the unknown. This fear, if you let it, prevents you from discovering the *real you*—the person inside who is waiting to start living! Don't delay, start building a structure that adds meaning to your life *today*.

8. DEVISE A SELF-CARE PLAN

These are the basic things your mother told you to do when you were a child: Get a good night's sleep, eat a well-balanced diet, and exercise regularly. A well-rested, nourished, fit body can withstand stress and illness much better that a tired, hungry, out-of-shape body (this is equally true for adults). Plan activities that are fun and make you feel good about yourself. Balance your life to include work, play, friendships, and family. Self-care is a primary building block to effective management of mental illness.

Unfortunately, many people define self-care as being selfish: "Jo, how can I set up a self-care plan? It means I have to drop something else and then my family's needs will not get met." Put a spin on this rationale and look what happens: If you don't take care of yourself, your family will have to deal with your increasing symptoms and the problems they create. Then their needs really go by the wayside. There are several important ingredients in a good self-care plan:

ESTABLISH HEALTHY DIET, SLEEP, AND EXERCISE PATTERNS

I can't overemphasize how important this is to physical and mental health! Make this a priority in your self-care plan or other efforts will be in vain.

RECOGNIZE YOUR PERSONAL STRESS CUES

Become aware of the stresses in your life and how they trigger symptoms of your illness. Have a daily stress reduction plan and during periods of excessive stress take action to eliminate nonessential burdens. Think of a boat taking on water—you need to cast unnecessary items overboard to preserve human lives. In this case you need to cast unnecessary tasks and commitments overboard to protect your mental health. After lightening your load use physical activity (walking, exercise, gardening, etc.), meditation, and humor to reduce the remaining stress. Give yourself permission to take "stress breaks" as needed and stop comparing yourself to others. Focus on your strengths and limitations, not on the strengths and limitations of others who may have very different life circumstances.

PARTIALIZE AND PRIORITIZE

Learn to address one problem at a time instead of trying to solve them all at once. Write down all the problems that are interfering with your recovery then number them from the most to least important. Pick the problem you identified as the most important and tackle it first. Once you resolve that problem, go on to the next. Staying focused on one problem at a time helps prevent stress overload and is *vital* to your mental health! It also provides opportunities for success. Each time you resolve a problem on your list it encourages you to keep on going.

ESTABLISH BOUNDARIES

Boundary setting means creating clear limits about what you will and will not/can and cannot do. Avoid the temptation to compare yourself with others. This requires an honest assessment of your time, energy, support networks, physical and emotional strengths and limitations, interests, and goals.

Remember boundaries should be flexible so they can be adjusted as life circumstances change.

AVOID THE ATLAS MYTH

The belief that you can manage everything alone is a dangerous myth. Reaching out in times of stress helps you become more independent because it helps you regroup and get back on your feet more quickly.

BABY STEPS

You will not always have the "right" answers and you will have "off" days. Patience and a genuine desire to cope more effectively with daily life pressures is an important step toward healthy living. What seems overwhelming and insurmountable frequently becomes manageable when broken down into a series of steps (see "Partialize and Prioritize").

REDISCOVER THE ART OF PLAY

Play is a wonderful way to recharge emotional batteries. Unfortunately, most adults have forgotten how to play or feel silly when they do indulge themselves. Sing songs, skip down the street, or play a favorite childhood game. Play reminds us that there is more to life than the "serious stuff" that defines most adult activities. This is especially important if you are coping with a chronic illness since this makes life even more serious.

CULTIVATE A SENSE OF HUMOR

Laughter reduces anxiety and reminds us that life is often unpredictable. Laughing at adversity helps us maintain balance and a sense of control—even when our ship is sinking (that is what lifeboats are for). Do *not* confuse humor with the mask identified in chapter 5 ("Tears of a Clown"). *Healthy* humor is used as a safety valve to reduce or redirect high levels of tension. It is time-limited and individuals who use humor for stress relief continue to seek out people with whom they can "be real." When humor becomes a mask for emotional pain it increases rather than decreases stress. Monitor your use of humor to make sure you are using it correctly.

MIXING THE INGREDIENTS

Review the self-care strategies identified above and select the ones that fit your life-style. A proper balance of these ingredients will result in less stress and a more positive outlook on life. By learning to accept and love yourself *because of* not *in spite of* who you are your self-care plan can become a priority!

9. ACQUIRE A WIDE RANGE OF COPING SKILLS

Develop skills to cope with symptoms of your illness. Taking an active role in symptom management significantly reduces negative consequences these symptoms create. Go to educational classes, lectures, workshops, and family programs. Attend support groups so you can practice new skills in safe surroundings. Read books, watch educational videos, talk to mental health professionals, seek out patients with your diagnosis who have already mastered the skills you are trying to learn. Be creative in applying skills so they become your own. Remember the more tools you have in your toolbox, the better your chances of interrupting symptoms before they interrupt you! Most important, don't forget to apply your coping skills once you develop them! A toolbox full of tools is worthless unless you use them. The more you practice, the better you get at applying coping skills when you need them most.

10. REEVALUATE SKILLS ON A REGULAR BASIS

Don't get too smug once you develop a set of coping skills that seem to be working well. Remember to evaluate your skills on a regular basis to see if they are still working. As you face new experiences, meet new challenges, and go through different stages of life, your coping skills need to grow and change with you. Coping skills, like clothing, get outdated and need to be replaced with up-to-date options. When you do replace existing coping skills don't throw the old ones away—save them for a rainy day! Like clothing, these skills may come back in style at some future date. You never know when old tricks may be just what you need to solve new problems.

11. GET HELP TO MANAGE FAMILY CONFLICTS

Chronic mental illness creates distress in even the healthiest families. Over time stress levels can undermine the loving support family members work so hard to create and hold onto. Individuals often get so caught up in their confusion and pain they cannot identify and work through problems, which interferes with family harmony. When this occurs seek help from mental health professionals trained in family therapy. A third party can usually restate feelings and needs so others can hear them without becoming defensive. Getting new ideas about how to manage chronic problems keeps family members from becoming burned out and frustrated. Like a relay race that depends on many runners to successfully navigate a course, when recovery becomes a "team effort" it reduces family distress and gives individual members opportunities to recover and regroup.

12. REALIZE YOU ARE GRIEVING A LOSS

Coming to terms with the fact that you or someone you love has a mental illness can be devastating. It gives rise to all nature of thoughts about what could have, might have, should have been. It challenges the affected individual and those who love him or her to face their own and society's beliefs about what having a mental illness means. This often creates profound sadness, since to admit an illness exists means coming to terms with what was, what is, and what can never be. This grief work *must* occur before those affected can move on to identify what might still be. Since family members grieve in different stages it often generates conflict. Mental health professionals can help families develop strategies to get through the loss together. Once families complete their initial grief work (other times of sadness will come as the illness progresses) they can focus on strengths and possibilities rather than limitations and losses.

13. BE PREPARED FOR THINGS TO GET WORSE BEFORE THEY GET BETTER

Yes, I *know*—this is the last thing you want to hear! As a therapist I feel obligated to warn my clients so there are no curve balls once they enter the recovery process. Therapy dredges up many painful memories that can temporarily increase emotional distress. An analogy might help you understand why it hurts more before it feels better. Think back to when you were a child. Remember when you cut yourself your mother put iodine or mercurochrome on the cut to reduce the risk of infection? It stung like the dickens at first but it helped the healing process begin. Likewise, when you have a cavity and go to the dentist, the repairs are often uncomfortable but the end result is a sound tooth. Psychiatric intervention is much the same. Therapists stir up feelings and memories in order to help you identify and work through them. Again, the remedy is initially painful but prepares the wound for healing. Pus in an infected sore must be drained before damaged tissue can repair itself. As long as the pus remains the wound continues to fester and worsen. So it is with emotional pain. Knowing this up front often gives clients the courage to face the pain created during the initial stages of therapy. It hurts more before it feels better, and the only way out is through. Forewarned is forearmed so now you know if you feel really bad in the beginning stages of recovery it is normal! As time passes the pain will gradually decrease as hope begins to creeping back into your life. Give it a try—you have nothing to lose and everything to gain. Take a risk! Face the demon that keeps you from removing your mask and becoming real. Once you get to the other side you just might like what and who you find.

14. PATIENCE IS A VIRTUE

Good things come to those who wait. Always keep in mind that recovery is a process. If you travel 50 miles down a road to get somewhere you must travel the same 50 miles in reverse to get back to where you started. Don't expect an overnight cure or instant recovery—they don't exist! Develop a hopeful and realistic attitude about the journey and set a pace you can live with. This reduces the temptation to give up, especially if progress is slow and painful. Think about how hard it is to keep dieting when you hit a plateau and don't lose any weight for 2 to 3 weeks. If you just hold on and keep plugging away, weight will gradually drop one pound at a time. In recovery time is your ally not your foe! It allows you to measure progress step by step instead of leap by leap. Remember that change is scary, and if you go too fast you run the risk of scaring yourself right back into patterns of unhealthy behavior. As the tortoise said to the hare, "Slow and steady wins the race."

15. KEEP ON TALKING

Remember that social isolation and stuffing feelings are primary risk factors in the relapse process. The surest way to set yourself up for a fall is to stop sharing how you feel with others. Be willing to honestly communicate your feelings, needs, and fears with people you trust and allow them to do the same. It is far more painful to hide from reality and present a front that others do not understand than to share your experiences and ask for their support.

16. CELEBRATE SUCCESSES ALONG THE WAY

Recovery is a process and should be celebrated one success at a time. How depressing and overwhelming to think we have to wait to the end of our lives to see if we succeeded. Consider each step you take in the direction of recovery to be one more piece of your puzzle now in place. Each piece bringing you closer to the finished product. Each time you handle a difficult situation better than you have in the past be sure to pat yourself on the back. Even if the outcome is not as positive as you had hoped if you even tried to redirect the outcome you deserve praise. Each attempt creates a stepping stone to the next phase of recovery. Even relapse provides opportunities to review current coping skills and make changes, as needed, to improve your responses in the future. Celebrate the journey *not* the destination since that is what life is all about.

I have identified 16 beginning tools for recovery that you may want to add to your toolbox. There are many more and I hope you will experiment with different ideas to customize your toolbox. As I have said many times, tools are only of value if you are willing to use them, have them repaired and replaced when necessary, and learn when and how to activate them. In closing this chapter let's review some basic facts about the recovery process. I hope these thoughts will help you remember how important it is to identify your mask, the risk factors that send you scurrying to put it on, and the value of developing and applying coping skills that move you closer to becoming real.

1. Mental illnesses, like many medical conditions, are "invisible" to casual observers. Because we cannot "see" the effects of these conditions until they reach an acute stage, we often find it difficult to believe they are real. Removing the mask that makes these illnesses so invisible is the first step to gaining the support and validation so desperately needed to successfully navigate the recovery process.

2. Because these conditions are invisible, symptoms are often ignored until a crisis occurs. Waving flags to alert ourselves and others that problems are brewing can prevent many crises and reduce the negative impact of those that do occur. This can only happen if you are willing to remove your mask.

3. When symptoms are ignored until the condition progresses to a crisis point, the recovery process is longer and more stressful for the individual and their family members. You just *thought* that mask was saving you and others from more pain. The reality: It *adds* even more pain to an already overloaded family system.

4. Lack of knowledge about one's mental illness and the symptoms it creates, feeling intimidated by medical professionals, and being afraid to accept a psychiatric diagnosis, frequently leads people to delay treatment. Remember *you* are in the driver's seat but you have to take off your mask in order to see where you are going.

5. Recovery is a *process* that occurs gradually across time. Although there is no cure for chronic mental illnesses, symptoms can be managed so individuals can lead more satisfying lives. You don't have to rip off your mask all at once! Plot a course and start moving—you'll be amazed how quickly you

move down the road toward becoming real. The key ingredients needed for this task are:

A.   Developing a knowledge base about your condition, its symptoms, possible treatments, and potential outcomes. The more you know, the less afraid you will be about becoming real.

B.   Include family members in treatment so they can better understand and cope with symptoms that affect family life. There's safety in numbers! The more family members know the easier it is to remove the mask. You may give them the courage needed so they too can remove their masks.

C.   Remember that the goal of treatment is symptom *management,* not cure. Once you realize flaws can make some things more beautiful, it will be easier to slip out from behind your mask.

D.   Be willing to experiment with different treatment options until the best combinations of interventions for your individual experience are identified (this may include but is not limited to medication, individual and/or group therapy, hospitalization, family therapy, and participation in community-based support groups and organizations). Becoming real requires a lot of false starts and stops—get all the help you can to get down this interesting and exciting road with as little pain as possible.

E.   Realize that relapse episodes (a temporary recurrence of symptoms) may occur when you experience stressful events in your life (anniversary dates, deaths, other losses, significant life changes). When relapses do occur, the goal is to identify and activate supports to reduce negative consequences (i.e., put your symptoms back into remission as quickly as possible). No matter what don't put your mask back on! You've come too far to go back to where you started.

F. Patients and family members are the *key players* in the recovery process! Your treatment team is only as useful as you allow them to be. A wheelbarrow with no one to push it is worthless—so is a therapist without a client's guidance of their interventions! Take off your mask so we can see who we're helping and what we can do to make your journey safer and less painful.

Now, let's move on to the final chapter of this book. This closing chapter explores the fact that human beings, by their very nature and complexity, are works in process from the moment of birth to the moment of death. We are always growing, changing, evolving, testing, challenging, questioning, learning, teaching, and striving to become the best selves we can be. Ready to take a closer look at this process as it unfolds? Turn the page and start reading!

CHAPTER 14

A WORK IN PROGRESS

I have loved science and biology since early childhood. I remember watching films in elementary school about different insects and how they create hives, colonies, and nests. I was especially fascinated by films about bees because I could never figure out how each bee knew its role: who collected pollen for honey, built new combs for the hive, cared for the eggs, became the queen. Somehow bees "know" exactly what is necessary to ensure the hive's survival. Human growth and development is equally fascinating. We start out as two small cells and grow into an organism with billions of cells. As the fetus develops cells "know" what they are destined to become and, when all goes as planned, in 9 months a perfect and tiny human being is born. Although miraculous, conception and birth are only the beginning of a journey called life. Individuals continue to grow and evolve physically, mentally, emotionally, and spiritually from conception until death. We rarely stop to think about what a wondrous gift each of our lives represents. This is especially true for those among us who are "different" because of physical, mental, or emotional disabilities. They are no less special or incredible but often *feel* inferior, like damaged goods that nobody wants, because somewhere in their development things "went wrong." Let's challenge this belief and see what happens.

181

My youngest son is hearing impaired so I am learning sign language. My teacher is from another state and some of her signs are different from those used in Texas. When she began teaching here, her elementary school students repeatedly made the sign for "wrong" when she made a sign that was different from how *they* signed it. She signed back to them, "No, not wrong—different!" We, as individuals, families, and society must begin to define those among us who are struggling with mental and emotional problems as "different" not "defective or wrong." Individuals with disabilities are *not* inferior, bad, undesirable, or damaged goods that should be put on the back shelf! They are people, like you and me, who carry a little extra lead in their saddlebags. They can still run a hell of a race, but have to be more creative about how they balance their load. Let's look at an example.

Earlier I mentioned the social work student who was paralyzed from the neck down except for limited use of his hands. This student could not even get out of bed without the help of an attendant. He was totally helpless *until* placed in his motorized wheelchair. I am a fitness nut and my greatest fear is becoming physically disabled; that is why I accepted this student! I shared my fear with him and he told me something that forever changed my thinking about what the words *handicapped* and *disabled really* mean. He said, "Jo, believe it or not, having a paralyzed body is not nearly as disabling as a bad attitude. When first injured I was angry, bitter, and lost all hope of living a normal life. As time passed, I began to realize that yes, I was physically disabled, but my *handicap* was the way I approached my disability. Once I realized my attitude was preventing me from reaching my potential I focused on creating ways to work with my strengths instead of lamenting over my limitations." He was honest in saying that at times he still feels angry and helpless; for example, when his attendant is late and he is trapped in bed until the attendant finally shows up. But he quickly reminds himself that his disability is only as handicapping as *he* allows it to be.

This man now has a master's degree in social work and helps other disabled people get on with their lives. He lives in his own apartment, has a specially designed van so he can drive, and has an active social life. The course of his life changed drastically when he broke his neck in a tragic accident, but, after grieving this loss, he *chose* to plot a course that gives meaning and purpose to his own life and the lives of others, like me, who are lucky enough to know him. I often share this story with my clients so they can see that yes, they are disabled, but the way they *approach* their disability can either be a challenge or a handicap: The *choice* is up to each of them (as it is for each of you)!

If we accept the notion that each individual is a work in progress from conception to death, it provides endless opportunities for personal growth and change. There is, however, a catch. From infancy we encounter different people whose actions and comments shape our self-image. If we are lucky the messages we receive create a positive self-image ("I'm smart, valuable, have a purpose in life"). Unfortunately, many people receive messages that contribute to a negative self-image ("I am stupid, ugly, worthless, a burden to my family and society"). In order to achieve our potential we must cast off the effect of messages that are destructive and replace them with practical alternatives. For an individual with disabilities this means constructing a life-style that allows them to make the most of their strengths. It means challenging "traditional" definitions of valuable and productive and creating new definitions that fit individual situations. Let's take a closer look at this issue.

As a society we place great emphasis on youth, beauty, physical fitness, and mental stability. We have become so rigid in using these standards to define what is right and good that individuals who are different become "unacceptable." This has a devastating effect on millions of individuals who cannot, no matter how hard they try, "fit" the existing image of what is right and good. The good news is that we can reverse this process by allowing individuals to be the unique beings they are.

First we must stop treating people like products that have to meet certain specifications. Human beings are not cars on an assembly line, cereal in a box, or eggs in a carton. We are more like a sampler of Whitman's chocolates *without* the "cheat sheet" that tells you what is inside each piece—you're never *really* sure what's inside until you take the first bite! If we can learn to define those who deviate from the norm as "different," not "defective or wrong," each of us benefits. We have so much to teach each other if only we can get past the stereotypes that provide us with excuses to avoid things we don't understand. This process requires each of us to take a closer look at who we are and why we react so defensively when others "differ" from our concept of "normal." What we often find is that the "differences" presented by others ignite our fears. My fear of being physically disabled was ignited when I worked with the disabled student I described above, but look how much I grew by pushing through my fear and saying "yes!"

Self-discovery and social change are both frightening and exciting because you never know what's on the other side of the hill unless you climb to the top. I think the biggest handicap we face as a society is our tendency to think about all the things that might go wrong if we tamper with the existing structure. Instead, we need to consider all the things that might go right if we dare to challenge what is and create something new! This means taking off our masks and being who we really are. Pursuing our talents and following our dreams. By challenging the existing structure, we free ourselves and others to pursue happiness and self-expression. If we follow our hearts and find balance and harmony by using the gifts God has given us, we become real.

Each of us has strengths and limitations. By focusing on our strengths we move closer to finding the person behind the mask. Being a work in progress is what becoming real is all about. To become real we must confront the fear and pain of leaving the uncomfortably familiar to make room for new discoveries about ourselves and our world. Self-acceptance is the ultimate reward of becoming real, and once achieved, can be passed on to others. Keep these thoughts in mind as you continue to move toward becoming real:

1. Life is like putting together a puzzle without a picture to guide you. Curiosity prompts you to keep adding pieces to see what you might discover. The pleasure of building a puzzle comes not from viewing the finished product but from seeing the picture unfold one piece at a time.

2. Learning to live with a disabling conditon is a bit like working for a bureaucracy. Just when you think you *finally* have it all figured out the rules change! Learn to roll with the punches and you will always either land on your feet or have a pillow to cushion your fall.

3. We can always enhance, add to, embellish, and better ourselves as long as we don't stop trying. This does not mean we should try to live up to social standards or be like everyone else! It means being the best person we can be by challenging ourselves to grow and learn for as long as we live.

4. Value is defined by individuals and what may seem insignificant to one is a rare treasure to another. When you feel hopeless, worthless, and insignificant remember that to someone, somewhere, you *do* make a difference. You may be the treasure in someone else's life.

5. Remember that differences keep life from becoming dull and predictable. Frame your disability as a challenge and use your strengths creatively to jump the hurdles life places in your path. A race won after great exertion is much more of a victory than a race won without effort.

6. Finally, the best teachers are those who have walked the walk. Be courageous in educating others about mental illness and the impact it has on individuals, families, and society. Remember the story I told in chapter 2 about the hardware man. He taught me a great deal about how important it is to allow others to choose for themselves even when *my* choices seem more appropriate. Take off your mask

and teach others what living with mental illness is *really* all about. Change has to start somewhere and it might as well be with you! Who knows, your contribution might influence social attitudes so someday individuals with mental illnesses will no longer need to wear masks—even in public.

EPILOGUE

When I began this book my husband said, "Jo, I think you're writing this book about yourself." In some ways he was right. I wrote the Preface on the 6th anniversary of my sister's death. Writing the book advanced my own recovery from this terrible loss. It was "time" to write it. It is written from my heart with the purpose of helping individuals affected by mental illness get the support and recognition they deserve. I have seen and experienced a great deal of pain and suffering generated by mental illness. These "no-fault" diseases gradually rob their victims of the ability to participate fully in families, the employment arena, social settings, and in society. Because their symptoms are often "invisible," they sacrifice themselves by participating in a deadly masquerade trying to fit in and be like everybody else. This seems a very high price to pay for a ticket into mainstream America.

Nobody would "choose" to have a mental illness. If we were at K-Mart and heard, "Attention K-Mart shoppers: blue light special in aisle 13. The first 50 customers will receive a mental illness of their choice at 50% off the regular price," how many of us would walk, much less run, to make sure we were one of the first 50 people to reach aisle 13? Most of us would run in the other direction as fast as possible! Individuals with mental illnesses do not ask to become ill and would gladly stand in a line marked "returns and exchanges" if this were possible. They do not "act sick" to get our attention—they *are* sick and would rather *not* be noticed. In the 10 years I have worked in psychiatry the statement I hear most often from my clients is,

187

"Jo, we just want to be at peace with ourselves. To have normal lives, whatever that means. We want people to believe we are really sick. We want to live our lives like everybody else, is that too much to ask?" Seems like a reasonable request to me—how about you?

Can we help individuals with mental illnesses move closer to achieving this goal? *Yes*, by educating ourselves and others about mental illness and how it affects millions of people each year. By encouraging those affected to remove their masks so we can see who they really are, and by avoiding the temptation to back away from those courageous enough to accept this challenge. By befriending these people and treating them like "one of us" because they are. By challenging the myths that perpetuate fear and feed social stigma. By remembering these individuals are somebody's child, sister, brother, friend, or parent. By remembering that each of them is a *real* human being with feelings, needs, hopes, and dreams just like the rest of us. By welcoming them into our fold with open arms and being willing to see them as "different" not "bad or defective." By remembering that any one of us could be any one of them and we too would crave acceptance and support from our fellow man. Think, I mean *really think*, about what I'm saying before you close this book. It may help save lives and change social attitudes. Change starts with one tiny idea that grows into a social movement. Please be a part of this process so we can, once and for all, end this deadly masquerade.

SUGGESTED READING LIST

This book, written in a self-help format, provides an overview of mental illness using personal accounts, examples, and analogies. The following reading list is provided for individuals interested in acquiring additional information about mental illness. I have arranged reading material by subject heading to streamline the process of locating books of interest pertaining to various types of mental illnesses.

ANXIETY AND PANIC DISORDERS

Archer, J. (1991). *Managing anxiety and stress* (2nd ed). Oakland, CA: LC.

Barlow, D. H. (1988). *Anxiety and its disorders: The nature and treatment of anxiety and panic.* New York: Guilford.

Bennis, J., & Barrada, A. (1994). *Embracing the fear: Learning to manage panic and anxiety attacks.* Center City, MN: Hazelden.

Bourne, E. (1990). *The anxiety and phobia workbook.* Oakland, CA: New Harbinger.

Craig, K. D., & Dobson, K. S. (1994). *Anxiety and depression in adults and children.* Oklahoma City: SAGE.

Farrell, M. (1994). *Unwind: Turkeys do fly.* Columbus, Ohio: C. J. Howie.

Gold, M. C. (1990). *Good news about panic anxiety and phobias.* New York: Bantam.

Handly, R. W. (1987). *Anxiety and panic attack: Their cause and cure.* New York: Fawcett.

Knowles, J. (1993). *What of the night? A journey through depression and anxiety.* Scottdale, PA: Herald.

Lark, S. (1993). *Anxiety and stress: A self-help program.* Los Altos, CA: National Nursing Review.

Maro, R. (1990). *Prisoner of fear: My long road to freedom from panic attacks, anxiety, and agoraphobia.* Canton, OH: Hickory Grove.

McCullough, C. J. (1994). *Managing your anxiety: Regaining control when you feel stressed, helpless, and alone.* Los Angeles: J. P. Tarcher.

Peuifoy, R. Z. (1995). *Anxiety, phobias and panic: A step-by-step program for regaining control of your life.* New York: Warner.

Wilson, R. R. (1987). *Don't panic: Taking control of anxiety attacks.* New York: HarpCollins.

Wolpe, J. M., & Wolpe, D. (1988). *Life without fear: Anxiety and its cure.* Oakland, CA: New Harbinger.

CHILD AND ADOLESCENT DISORDERS

Barkley, R. A. (1995). *Taking care of ADHD: The complete, authoritative guide for parents.* New York: Guilford.

Hallowell, E., Halowell, J., & Rately, J. (1994). *Driven to distraction.* New York: Pantheon.

Husain, S. A., & Kashani, J. (Eds.).(1991). *Anxiety disorders in children and adolescents.* Washington, DC: American Psychiatric Association.

Kerns, L., & Lieberman, A. (1993). *Helping your depressed child.* Rocklin, CA: Prima.

Russell, M. L. (1993). *Planning for the future: Providing a meaningful life for a child with disability.* Evanson, IL: American.

Russell, M. L. (1995). *The life planning workbook.* Evanson, IL: American.

Wender, P. (1987). *The hyperactive child, adolescent, and adult: Attention deficit disorder throughout the lifespan.* New York: Oxford University Press.

Dual Diagnosis

Backus, W. (1994). *Learning to tell myself the truth: A 12-week guide to freedom from anger, anxiety, depression.* Minneapolis, MN: Bethany.

Dowling, C. (1992). *You mean I don't have to feel this way? New help for depression, anxiety, and addiction.* New York: Simon & Schuster.

Evans, K., & Sullivan, M. (1990). *Dual diagnosis: Counseling the mentally ill substance abuser.* New York: Guilford.

Heston, L. (1992). *Mending minds.* New York: W. H. Freeman.

Minkoff, K., & Drake, R. E. (1992). *Dual diagnosis of major mental illness and substance abuse disorder.* San Francisco: Jossey-Bass.

Torrey, E. (1994). *Schizophrenia and manic depressive disorder: The biological roots of mental illness as revealed by the landmark study of identical twins.* New York: Basic Books.

Major Depression/Manic Depression (Bipolar Disorder)

Copeland, M. (1992). *The depression workbook.* Oakland, CA: New Harbinger.

Copeland, M. (1994). *Living without depression and manic depression: A workbook for maintaining mood stability.* Oakland, CA: New Harbinger.

Duke, P., & Hockman, G. (1992). *A brilliant madness: Living with manic depressive illness.* New York: Bantam.

Goodwin, F., & Jamison, K. (1990). *Manic depressive illness.* New York: Oxford University Press.

Hamilton, D. (1995). *Sad days, glad days: A story about depression.* Mortin Grove, IL: Whitman.

Jamison, K. (1995). *An unquiet mind: A memoir of moods and madness.* New York: Random.

Klein, D., & Wender, P. (1993). *Understanding depression: A complete guide to its diagnosis and treatment.* New York: Oxford University Press.

Manning, M. (1995). *Undercurrents: A life beneath the surface.* San Francisco: Harper SF.

Miscellaneous Topics

American Psychiatric Association (1994). *Diagnostic and statistical manual of mental disorders* (4th ed.). Washington, DC: American Psychiatric Association.

Bouricius, J. K. (1996). *Psychoactive drugs and their effects on mentally ill persons.* Arlington, VA: National Alliance for the Mentally Ill.

Coates, R. (1990). *A street is not a home: Solving America's homeless dilemma.* Del Mar, CA: Prometheus.

Dickens, R., & Marsh, D. (1994). *Anguished voices: Personal accounts of siblings and children of people with mental illness.* Boston: Center of Psychiatric Rehabilitation.

Govig, S. D. (1994). *Souls are made of endurance: Surviving mental illness in the family.* Louisville, KY: Westminster John Knox.

Hatfield, A. B. (1984). *Coping with mental illness in the family: A family guide.* Arlington, VA: NAMI.

Hatfield, A. B. (1991). *Coping with mental illness in the family: A family guide.* New York: Guilford.

Hatfield, A. B., & Lefley, H. (1993). *Surviving mental illness: Stress, coping, adaptation.* New York: Guilford.

Lamb, R. (1992). *Treating the homeless mentally ill.* Washington, DC: American Psychiatric Association.

Lickey, M. E., & Gordon, B. (1991). *Medicine and mental illness: The use of drugs in psychiatry.* New York: W. H. Freeman.

Norden, M. J. (1995). *Beyond Prozac: Antidotes for modern times.* New York: HarpCollins.

Olson, L. S. (1994). *He was still my daddy: Coming to terms with mental illness.* New York: Ogden.

Schiller, L. (1994). *The quiet room: A journey out of the torment of madness.* New York: Warner.

Sheehan, S. (1982). *Is there no place on Earth for me?* Boston: Houghton-Mifflin.

Torrey, E. (1988). *Nowhere to go: The tragic odyssey of the homeless mentally ill.* New York: Harper & Row.

Turnball, J. R. (1989). *Disability and the family: A guide to decisions for adulthood.* Baltimore, MD: Paul H. Brooks.

Wahl, O. F. (1995). *Media madness: Images of mental illness.* New Brunswick, NJ: Rutgers University Press.

Wasnow, M. (1995). *Skipping stones: The rippling effects of mental illness in the family.* Palo Alto, CA: Science & Behavior Books.

Woolis, R. (1992). *When someone you love has a mental illness: A handbook for family, friends, and caregivers.* Los Angeles: J. P. Tarcher.

Yudofsky, S. C., & Ferguson, T. (1991). *What you need to know about psychiatric drugs.* New York: Ballantine.

Wrobleski, A. (1994). *Suicide survivors: A guide for those left behind* (2nd ed.). Minneapolis, MN: Afterwards.

Wrobleski, A. (1995). *Suicide, Why? Eighty-five questions and answers about suicide* (2nd ed.). Minneapolis, MN: Afterward.

OBSESSIVE–COMPULSIVE DISORDER

Kernodle, W. (1993). *Panic disorder: What you don't know may be dangerous to your health* (2nd ed.). Richmond, VA: Kernodle.

Rapoport, J. L. (1989). *The boy who couldn't stop washing: The experience and treatment of obsessive compulsive disorder.* New York: NAL/Dutton.

Ross, J. (1994). *Triumph over fear.* New York: Bantam.

POSTTRAUMATIC STRESS DISORDER

Averill, J. R., Catlin, G., & Chon, K. K. (1990). *Rules of hope.* New York: Springer-Verlag.

Bass, E., & Davis, L. (1988). *The courage to heal: A guide for women survivors of child sexual abuse.* New York: Harper & Row.

Beesley, S. W. (1989). *Vietnam: The heartland remembers.* New York: Berkley.

Bourne, P. G. (1970). *Men, stress, and Vietnam.* Boston: Little Brown.

Braza, J., & Braza, K. (1991). *War and its aftermath.* Hawthorne, NJ: Career Press.

Brende, J. O., & Parson, E. R. (1985). *Vietnam veterans: The road to recovery.* New York: Plenum.

Catherall, D. R. (1992). *Back from the brink: A family guide to overcoming traumatic stress.* New York: Bantam.

Figley, C. R., & Leventman, S. (1980). *Strangers at home: Vietnam veterans since the war.* New York: Preager.

Finkelhor, D., Gelles, R. J., & Hotaling, G. T. (1983). *The dark side of families.* Beverley Hills, CA: Sage.

Flannery, R. B. (1992). *Posttraumatic stress disorder: The victim's guide to healing and recovery.* New York: Crossroad.

Frankl, V. E. (1962). *Man's search for meaning.* New York: Simon & Schuster.

Grubman-Black, S. D. (1990). *Broken boys/mending men.* Blue Ridge Summit, PA: Tals Books.

Herman, J. L. (1992). *Trauma and recovery.* New York: Basic Books.

Kuenning, D. A. (1991). *Life after Vietnam: How veterans and their loved ones can heal the psychological wounds of war.* New York: Paragon.

Mason, P. (1990). *Recovering from the war.* High Springs, FL: Patience Mason.

Matsak, A. (1991). *When the bough breaks.* Oakland, CA: New Harbinger.

Matsak, A. (1992). *I can't get over it: A handbook for trauma survivors.* Oakland, CA: New Harbinger.

Moss, D. C. (1991). *The trauma trap.* Garden City, NY: Doubleday.

Palmer, L. (1987). *Shrapnel in the heart.* New York: Random House.

Pennebaker, J. W. (1990). *Opening up: The healing power of confiding in others.* New York: Avon.

Schafer, R. (1992). *Retelling a life.* New York: Basic Books.

SCHIZOPHRENIA

Arieti, S. (1979). *Understanding and helping the schizophrenic: A guide for family and friends.* New York: Simon & Schuster.

Backlar, P. (1994). *The family face of schizophrenia.* Los Angeles: J. P. Tarcher.

Bernheim, K., & Levine, R. (1979). *Schizophrenia: Symptoms, causes, treatments.* New York: W. W. Norton.

Bernheim, K., Levine, R., & Beale, C. (1982). *The caring family.* New York: Random House.

Deveson, A. (1991). *Tell me I'm here: One family's experience with schizophrenia.* New York: Viking Penguin.

Keefe, R. (1994). *Understanding schizophrenia: A guide to the new research on causes and treatment.* New York: Free Press.

Mueser, K., & Gingerich, S. (1994). *Coping with schizophrenia: A guide for families.* Oakland, CA: New Harbinger.

Park, C., & Shapiro, L. (1976). *You are not alone: Understanding and dealing with mental illness.* Boston: Little, Brown.

Torrey, E. (1983). *Surviving schizophrenia: A family manual.* New York: Harper & Row.

Torrey, E. (1995). *Surviving schizophrenia: For families, consumers, and providers* (3rd ed.). New York: HarpCollins.

Tsuang, M. (1983). *Schizophrenia: The facts.* New York: Oxford University Press.

Vine, P. (1982). *Families in pain: Children, sibling, spouses and parents of the mentally ill speak out.* New York: Pantheon.

Wasow, M. (1982). *Coping with schizophrenia: A survival manual for parents, relatives, and friends.* Palo Alto, CA: Science & Behavior.

Relapse Prevention

Beck, A. (1988). *Love is never enough.* New York: Harper & Row.

Clancy, J. (1996). *Anger and addiction: Breaking the relapse cycle, a teaching guide for professionals.* Madison, CT: Psychosocial Press.

Clancy, J. (1997). *Anger and relapse: Breaking the cycle.* Madison, CT: Psychosocial Press.

Daley, D. (1988). *Relapse prevention.* Bradenton, FL: Human Services Institute.

Ellis, A., & Becker, I. (1982). *A guide to personal happiness.* North Hollywood, CA: Wilshire.

Gorski, T. (1992). *The staying sober workbook.* Independence, MO: Herald House/Independence Press.

Gorski, T., & Miller, M. (1986). *Staying sober: A guide for relapse prevention.* Independence, MO: Herald House/Independence Press.

Mahoney, M. J., & Thoresen, C. E. (1974). *Self-control: Power to the person.* Monterey, CA: Brooks/Cole.

Marlatt, G. A., & Gordon, J. (Eds.). (1985). *Relapse prevention: A self-control strategy for the maintenance of behavior change.* New York: Guilford.

STARTING POINTS FOR HELP

Thousands of programs exist to help the mentally ill and those who love them. Two national agencies, listed below, act as clearinghouses for information on current books and films, research, and programs available to help the mentally ill and their families at the local, state, and national level. One phone call will get you moving in the right direction. *Make the call today!*

1. The National Mental Health Association
   1021 Prince Street
   Alexandria, Virginia 22314-2971
   (703) 838-7534

2. The National Alliance for the Mentally Ill
   200 North Glebe Road #1015
   Arlington, Virginia 22203-3754
   1-800-950-6264 (NAMI helpline)
   (703) 524-7600 ext. 7957

GOOD LUCK!!

About the Author

Jo Clancy, LMSW-ACP, LCDC received her bachelor's degree in Psychology from the University of Houston-Clear Lake in 1985 and her master's in Social Work from the University of Houston-Central Campus in 1987. She achieved advanced standing in Social Work in 1992 and concurrently received licensure as a Chemical Dependency Counselor. Ms. Clancy is employed full-time in the Houston Veterans Affairs Medical Center Trauma Recovery Program, is an adjunct faculty member at the University of Houston Graduate School of Social Work, and a Clinical Instructor in the Department of Psychiatry and Behavioral Sciences at Baylor College of Medicine. Her primary interests involve working with angry, chronically relapsing addicts and alcoholics and with clients and family members affected by psychiatric illness. Committed to teaching others how to conduct this work, she is a regular workshop presenter on local, state, National, and International levels. Jo is currently working on her fourth book *What Love Is: Lessons from the Heart,* a self-help book for individuals striving to create healthier more loving relationships in their lives.